BOOK EIGHT

2020

IMPEACH

V

HISTORY

BOOK EIGHT

2020

IMPEACH

V

HISTORY

Books may be ordered through booksellers or by contacting:
www.createspace.com/B084L26523
www.Amazon.com

———————————

CreateSpace Title ID: B084L26523

Jacked Design & Illustrations © Guebres Studios

ISBN-13: 9798610886541 *(sc)*
ISBN-10: ########## (ebk)

Printed in the United States of America
CreateSpace date: 02/02/2020

It all begins with ancestor worship –
our knowledge that they lived and died,
but with the need to believe
that they could overcome death and live again –
continue to live and watch over us.
– Opening to "Grandpa was a Deity"

--

–

"Az ikh vel zayn vi yener,
"If I am to be like someone else,
ver vet zayn vi ikh?"
who will be like me?"

--

Prologue Trump Card Book-8.

The world is awash with truth and lies, often the lies are easier to accept than the truth. Psychologists have devoted their careers to trying to explain why that is, we can simply accept it to be so.

Before I began this series, I was doing my family genealogy – it turned out I discovered some of the neat stuff Ancestry.com uses in its advertisements. In my case, it began with finding my – and had discovered I shared a grandparent with Thomas Jefferson.

Naturally, that piqued my interest, and I began to wonder if my line had other connections – the result was a book published within days of Trump's Inauguration. It had a practical limit, 1575 was the earliest year because it allowed the capture of sibling kinship between Virginia and Massachusetts colonists.

It turned out Burke's Peerage published a vaguely related work, but regular genealogies allowed me to discover the 4-Sisters and then create the chart on the print edition cover for this book. Based on the historic pattern published in January 2017, it was clear Trump was in for a contentious presidency; the 4-Sisters affirmed his victory over Hillary was inevitable; it also shows why the Impeachment had to fail.

History repeats until a revolution or catastrophic event occurs to disrupt it. In keeping with history, there are a few who could defeat Trump in 2020 – Bernie Sanders, Mike Bloomberg, Thomas Steyer, and Amy Klobuchar are among them.

Even if they weren't baseless for lack of a statutory or otherwise clearly defined crime or action, the Impeachment efforts had to fail. It certainly didn't help that the House prosecutors were dishonest and lied about the alleged evidence, or went out of their way to defend the illegal actions of Joe Biden.

As a lifelong Democrat, it would be nice to see my Party control all three branches of government. But as an American whose roots extend back before the Mayflower, it would be nice to see the nation survive as a superpower throughout its second 57-quadrennial cycle. And in that period we are likely to see a Progressive agenda of the type Theodore Roosevelt would approve and his cousin Franklin attempted to achieve with the New Deal.

Other books I've written over the past two decades have led me to believe achieving these things only requires the Democrats to seek goals rather than power.

When Impeachment versus History, History always wins.

When you can convict without a crime,
there are no Rules to guide the Rule of Law.

CHAPTERS

1	CHAPTER 01	....	*To Trial*
15	CHAPTER 02	....	*Biden Hoax*
29	CHAPTER 03	....	*Grow Up*
41	CHAPTER 04	....	*Gearbox*
53	CHAPTER 05	....	*The Big Lie*
65	CHAPTER 06	....	*Investigate*
81	CHAPTER 07	....	*SOTU 2020*
95	CHAPTER 08	....	*Verdict*
105	CHAPTER 09	....	*Candidates*
119	CHAPTER 10	....	*Pandemic*
131	CHAPTER 11	....	*Nuance*
143	CHAPTER 12	....	*FUN Begins*

MEMO: UNDERSTANDING CONGRESS
"It is difficult to get a man to understand something
when his salary depends upon his not understanding it."
- Upton Beall Sinclair (1878-1968)

CHAPTER ONE – TO TRIAL
"A hundred suspicions don't make a proof."
~ Fyodor Dostoyevsky, Crime and Punishment

Trump is a curious entity, and reality revealed in the praise that marks the opening remarks of the multi-part documentary entitled, *"Biography: The Trump Dynasty,"* included a sentence that declared: *"Trump is the Zeitgeist of America."*

Zeitgeist is one of those weird all-encompassing German terms that become popular and define various eras of history. It is a term that encompasses two ideas "Zeit" and "geist," meaning time and spirit. It is a spiritual atmosphere that ebbs and flows through society. Here the term refers to that general intellectual, moral, and cultural climate which defines or identifies the spirit of a generation, a period, and an era that might certainly prove critical to history.

That he is referred to in this manner establishes a subliminal recognition of the reality that we are at the beginning of a new era – one defined by a cycle of 57 four year periods, where the span from George Washington to his tenth cousin Barack Obama was marked by a first and a first. Now we have a new first, a creator of first times.

Think about the fact that Barbara Res was the first woman to run the construction of a major skyscraper – it was in New York City and called The Trump Tower. As mentioned in earlier books in this series, Trump respects women and their abilities; therefore he is the one that the Feminists attack so that they can ask some chauvinist pig politician for the rights Trump has gone out of his way to give women.

Trump told Res: *"Men are better than women, but one woman is better than ten good men."* And we see this in the global role Ivanka Trump played in the administration. We also see it in Melania Trump and her role as an independent First Lady. For Res, it was building the tallest concrete building in the City of New York, and for America, the topping off celebration showed Trump dealing with adversaries – the Mayor of New York, Ed Koch, had to sued by Trump before he could get the statutory Tax Abatement to which he was entitled. But, when they topped off the structure, it was Trump talking to Putin, Kim, Xi, or any of the others with whom, as President, he confronted – the rule is, everyone was friendly and the credit was shared.

But Trump today is not the Donald of 1991, who was immersed

in the divorce from Ivana and having a baby daughter – Tiffany – with Marla Maples; at the same time the Recession had killed Atlantic City and the excessively costly Taj Mahal Casino in Atlantic City. But then Trump was taught a new lesson – he was too big to fail. He reached an ideal point in "the art of the deal' where you get to dictate to those who have power over you.

The divorce had finalized and he married Marla Maples – it was time to *go public* and the stock market bailed him out at a profit – a stock that sold for $35 went to $0.17; Trump made millions.

Ultimately, *the art of the deal* is to win, even when you lose.

Trump had lost big, but also discovered he could win big by losing, getting knocked down, and then getting up to knock the other guy down – so long as he made sure the other guy didn't get up again.

The marriage to Marla folded, but he had Tiffany – the strong POTUS COUSIN who, in the Trump portion of *Jonathon's POTUS COUSINS* [JPC] I credited with providing the winning element that would make him President. But, Trump himself is a legitimate member of the ruling clan, he's a legitimate American Levite, but he's from the pre-1575 branch of the family while Marla is the post-1575 branch.

As we approach the 2020 election this ancestral connection will confront members of the family. When he confronted Hillary, he was facing an outsider married to a POTUS COUSIN – which might serve to explain Bill Clinton's *Oral in the Oval*, but certainly explains why Hillary lost. No one who isn't a POTUS COUSIN can serve in the Oval and expect the nation to survive.

People don't want to believe that; they deny Climate Change; they believe the House proved its impeachment case; they accepted that Schiff had irrefutable evidence of Trump-Russia collusion – and then they accepted Schiff's rendition of the Ukraine phone call over the actual transcript. They have always existed; they are the masses depicted in *The Emperor's New Clothes*, the lemmings running over the cliff because the one in front of them did.

The Trump name or brand-name trades on the lemmings that buy designer items, paying excessive premiums for the name and not the value of the product. But then you also have product knock-offs – the brand-name lookalike which makes you seem a lemming but has shown you to be among the financially wise – though, it makes you '*a deceiver of men/people'*. There are times, as Trump knows, deceiving people can be both harmless and profitable.

Knock-offs are interesting. Ronald Reagan used *Make America Great* as his campaign slogan – but it was in 2008 that we see Donald Trump trademark the slogan. It was a knock-off, what some might refer to as plagiarism, and it worked and will keep working because the heartland of America wants a great nation. It's only the New York or California elite who are trying to destroy America by ignoring the emotional gap that Trump fills.

When we look at the impeachment we see how deeply ingrained in the human spirit it is to lie to ourselves so that we can lie to others. Those who are being lied to fall into two groups. The first accepts and promotes the lie as if it were a truth that they alone realized; a second consists of those who attack the ones talking nonsense while enjoying the fact that they do. This group knows that it is through error that we arrive at the truth.

You are free to talk nonsense if it is your nonsense. It is your right to be wrong, but be so because it is your mistake to own, not because you are trying to please or gain the approval of another – one who is making a fool of you for their personal or political gain.

When the soul of a person has been attacked, when they realize they have been made the fool, they take refuge in sarcasm or childish emulating of the name or manners of others. This realization will, we can assume, overcome the minds and spirits of the wise, while the ignorant will bask in that ignorance and turn it to vented hatred – the kind that sees people destroy their own property because they are at odds with the actions of others.

We witnessed a variation of this with Nancy Pelosi deciding to deny House prosecutors the time necessary to familiarize themselves with any factual evidence.

When on 18 December the Articles of Impeachment were approved by the House, Pelosi declared she would not deliver those Articles to the Senate; she, therefore, did no need to appoint managers to preside over the House case and present their hearsay based assertions that Trump committed the very actions Joseph Biden proudly bragged about doing when in January 2018 he both boasted of it and implicated Obama in his criminal acts, by asserting: "*I'm leaving in six hours, you've got six hours. If you don't fire that prosecutor, United States will not give you $1 Billion in Aid...*" And when they correctly said he lacked that authority, he declared, "*if you don't trust me call the president.*"

When Clinton was impeached, the House Speaker used the two weeks of winter recess to appoint and prepare the prosecutors. With Pelosi, the delay was intended to extract assurances from McConnell that the terms of the trial would ensure the same nonsense the nation witnessed in the House – crime "*du jour*", "*de l'heure*", "*sans aucun*".

The nation has borne witness to former federal prosecutor, now Representative, Adam B Schiff lie about having evidence of collusion with Russia, then lie about the content or substance of Ukraine phone call, he has doubtless built a whole career on his ability to lie when he should be presenting facts. When Pelosi announced she would have the Articles of Impeachment to the Senate around 18 January, it was assumed Schiff would be appointed to present misrepresentation and lies to the Senators.

It was assumed Representative Schiff would be joined, or lead, by Representative Jerrold Nadler. When Clinton was tried, there were 13 white male managers sent to the Senate. On 14 January 2020, the Democratic Debate presented an all-white contingent featuring Bernie Sanders, Joe Biden, Elizabeth Warren, and Pete Buttigieg – along with Senator Amy Klobuchar and billionaire activist Tom Steyer. Thus the states represented are Vermont, Virginia, Massachusetts, Indiana, and then Minnesota – with Steyer representing the California-New York City billionaire cabal.

The impeachment game was complicated by Pelosi threatening to delay the transfer of Articles to the Senate. She appears to have been pulling a Biden threatening to pull the loan guarantee funds – it was extortion to get the Senate to obey what she wanted to be done.

Pelosi had no legal right to delay the transfer, but, based on the Clinton model – where the vote was 19 December and the Senate got the Articles on 6 January – she wasn't delaying anything. She was just lying to the media and public to pressure the Senate into rigging the Hearing and becoming a Kangaroo Court.

The voted Articles of Impeachment are based on-air when they should be a legal Wall or Fence that is clearly defined by statute and the courts.

ARTICLE I: ABUSE OF POWER. This is a charge that can be shown and established when an individual asserts they can perform in a manner clearly delineated and defined as being vested in another – Joe Biden bragged of crossing this line when he asserted the authority to terminate the Billion Dollar loan guarantee Congress appropriated to secure a Ukrainian ability to purchase supplies to defend against a Russian incursion after its Crimean annexation. In that case, it was a threatened violation of *The Impoundment Control Act of 1974.*

Among the stated charges is an assertion: "*Using the powers of his high office, President Trump solicited the interference of a foreign government, Ukraine, in the 2020 United States Presidential election.*"

However, the President is required to both enforce treaties and uphold the law. Biden's bragging of violating the law while holding the Office of Vice President mandates investigation; in that context, the Clinton era *Treaty with Ukraine on Mutual Legal Assistance in Criminal Matters* which was signed at Kyiv on July 22, 1998, provides the basis for the request to flag data mentioning the Bidens within the context of the ongoing Burisma corruption investigations. That data, in accordance with the treaty, to be forwarded to the Attorney General.

Of course, anything which eliminated Biden from consideration as the Democratic Party 2020 nominee would affect the election – by eliminating the nomination of a self-confessed criminal and opening the door to viable and honest candidates who, upon winning, would not be subject to immediate impeachment and conviction based on the obvious evidence of the C-SPAN recorded confession.

The first-hand witnesses verified the phone call transcript. And the invocation of data going to the Attorney General validates that it was invoking the treaty. Even the announcement of the investigation, which would be politically consistent with announcing that a Ukraine election promise was being kept, served the purpose of ensuring that the Democrats nominated an honest individual and not one mired in a history of corruption and using his son as a vehicle for laundering money deemed corrupt when paid directly.

ARTICLE II: OBSTRUCTION OF CONGRESS, can only be seen as a vague and undefined assertion without merit. The House asserts, rightly, that it has the power to impeach. In that regard, America was able to watch as Adam Schiff hide the operations of his committee in a Congressional sub-basement, where they could hide their operations from public view. There were complaints about a lack of transparency which denoted the existence of both illegal intent and practice.

When the hearings were made public, all the witnesses legally required to appear did – those who had a defense against appearance could have been brought to court and compelled, but House managers declined to exercise that option without any obstruction.

America witnessed the investigators rely on hearsay and gossip within a mixing bowl of unfounded supposition or inference. There is no hint of obstruction – the Impeachment moved at the pace set by the House, and after the affirmative vote, it was the Speaker of House who stopped or obstructed the process through her immediate refusal to honor a Constitutional obligation to appoint managers as prosecutors and forward the approved Articles to the Senate for trial.

In her attempt to prevent the Senate from moving forward in a timely and efficient manner, Nancy Pelosi, as House Speaker, was obstructing the workings of the Senate and thereby fully obstructing Congress. Assuming she were to run for re-election on 3 November, Pelosi would be 80-years-old, and offer 12th district California Voters the right to affirm they approve of her Obstruction of Congress and are of a mind consistent with having, in 1946, gave us Richard Nixon who was six-year-old Nancy's role model.

If we look at Pelosi's comment on her initial claim: *"No, I'm not holding them indefinitely. I will turn them over when I'm ready, and that will probably be soon."*

But, that statement was made on 9 January, when she already two days behind a transfer president set in the Clinton Impeachment – New York City Swamp Denizen Senator Chuck Schumer was in the Senate objecting to the bipartisan procedures established for Clinton. Schumer wanted a rigged hearing in which the testimony and witness hearsay assertions preceded reading or determination of the Charges any were to be testifying to.

With Clinton, the process initiated by the house vote ran from 19 December 1998 to 12 February 1999 – the next election was 2020. Now they have delayed what should have begun with the 18 December 2019 vote and, with all necessary witness testimony, ended by Friday, 14 February (based on the Clinton Trial ending on a Friday).

Super Tuesday represents the date when the greatest number of U.S. states hold primary elections and caucuses; in 2020, it will be on 3 March. Pelosi and Schumer had conspired in an effort to delay the Senate Trial, thereby keeping Warren and Sanders trapped in Washington until after Democrats abroad, American Samoa and

Alabama, Arkansas, California, Colorado, Maine, Massachusetts, Minnesota, North Carolina, Oklahoma, Tennessee, Texas, Utah, Vermont, and Virginia, had all voted for the Democratic nominee.

Leading to Super Tuesday, and influencing the outcome, were the 3 February Iowa Caucus, 11 February New Hampshire Primary, 22 February Nevada Caucus and 29 February South Carolina Primary – meaning the actions by Pelosi and Schumer were intentionally and pro-actively influencing 18 states or 36% of the nomination process.

Where there is no clearly delineated crime or wrongdoing, the idea of witnesses presents as an intention to introduce speculation as to intent or a review of suggested actions and justifications that has nothing to do directly with the actual action as supported by both law and treaty.

Apart from those whose criminal deeds are mentioned in the Articles and are related to Ukraine corruption investigation – namely Joseph Biden and his son Hunter Biden – there were no other primary witnesses. Any additional witnesses would, of necessity, deal with the criminality revealed in Joe Biden's braggadocious confession captured by the C-SPAN cameras in January 2018 and the criminality known to be associated with Burisma Holdings where Hunter Biden was on the Board of Directors.

Leading into the Debate, Electoral College projections had the Democrats with 248 votes and Republicans 204 – but that's without any knowledge of who the Democratic Nominee would be, so it meant the election became the Democrats to lose based on Florida, which the Republicans must win under this projection.

So what game was Pelosi playing?

In December, Pelosi's daughter Christine said, "*Don't mess with Nancy.*" Elaborating, Christine repeated the assertion and turned it back on the President: "*I'd say, Mr. President, don't mess with Nancy. Understand she is a prayerful, strong woman and if you might be feeling nervous or a meltdown or insecure, you don't need to do a self-diagnosis and project that onto somebody else.*"

But Christine was echoing her mother using it in the context of her religion: "*I don't hate anybody. I was raised in a Catholic house, we don't hate anybody — not anybody in the world. So don't you accuse me of any [hate]. As a Catholic I resent you using the word 'hate' in a sentence that addresses me,*" she continued. "*I pray for the president all the time. So don't mess with me when it comes to words like that."*

Of course, as the father and grandfather to Orthodox Jews, the idea of being a Catholic – those whose hate created the basis for the Inquisitions which evolved and yielded the Holocaust under Hitler – is not something Trump might accept. Especially when it was Trump who was the first POTUS to recognize Jerusalem as the lawful capital of Israel – thus fulfilling various prophecies two years before Pelosi's remarks.

Since the 2016 election results were announced, the world has witnessed interesting things in Congress. One such thing was the 30 hours of testimony given by – or demanded from – Donald Trump Jr. That involved an unsolicited half-hour meeting.

But Joseph R. Biden brags about violating multiple Federal Law Articles under 18USC and it is known that his son Hunter made millions in a do-nothing position with Burisma Holdings – a firm that is the target of multiple Ukraine corruption investigations involving international money laundering and crimes which have its owner "on the lamb" to avoid spending the rest of his life in prison – and yet there has not been a single minute of Congressional time devoted to investigating Biden involvement in the international criminal actions.

Interestingly, in the first week of November 2019, several news reports alleged: *"that the Ukrainian gas company, Burisma, that employed Democratic presidential candidate Joe Biden's son, Hunter Biden, pressed the Obama administration to end the corruption allegations against them during the 2016 election year."*

As documented by investigative reporter John Solomon, on 22 May 2015, Hunter Biden had emailed his father's longtime trusted aide and national security adviser, Deputy Secretary of State Antony Blinken saying: *"Have a few minutes next week to grab a cup of coffee? I know you are impossibly busy, but would like to get your advice on a couple of things, Best, Hunter."*

On 2 February 2016, Prosecutor General Viktor Shokin – the man Biden had used extortion to get fired – had authorized a court-ordered seizure of Burisma Holdings founder Mykola Zlochevsky's home and other valuables, including a luxury car. In anticipation of the corruption investigation reaching his American interests, in the spring of 2014, Zlochevsky had hired Hunter Biden and Devon Archer to be on his Board of Directors.

In February 2016, a meeting between a representative from Burisma Holdings and Undersecretary of State Catherine A. Novelli had been requested that invoked the Biden name and connection.

John Solomon reported: *"Just three weeks before Burisma's overture to State, Ukrainian authorities raided the home of the oligarch who owned the gas firm and employed Hunter Biden, a signal the long-running corruption probe was escalating in the middle of the U.S. presidential election. Hunter Biden's name, in fact, was specifically invoked by the Burisma representative as a reason the State Department should help, according to a series of email exchanges among U.S. officials trying to arrange the meeting."*

According to the report, and documented by State Department emails, fellow board member and business partner of Hunter Biden, Devon Archer met with Secretary of State John Kerry on 2 March 2016 – this was the day after Novelli was to meet with a former member of the Clinton administration, Karen Tramontano. From an internal State Department email dated 24 February 2016 we learn:

"Per our conversation, Karen Tramontano of Blue Star Strategies requested a meeting to discuss with U/S Novelli USG remarks alleging Burisma (Ukrainian energy company) of corruption. She noted that two high profile U.S. citizens are affiliated with the company (including Hunter Biden as a board member). Tramontano would like to talk with U/S Novelli about getting a better understanding of how the U.S. came to the determination that the company is corrupt. According to Tramontano there is no evidence of corruption, has been no hearing or process, and evidence to the contrary has not been considered. Would appreciate any background you may be able to provide on this issue and suggested TPs for U/S Novelli's meeting."

Apart from Tramontano, Blue Star employed another Clinton administration alumni, Sally Painter, and in the period when Ukraine investigations had been disrupted by the prosecutor firing both were working with New York-based criminal defense attorney John Buretta to settle America side of the Ukraine cases against Burisma.

It is rather interesting that, three years later, President Trump would be impeached for enquiring into the corruption that those who were seeking the State Department meeting sought to have suppressed – a meeting which occurred just prior to the event Biden bragged about when he boasted before C-SPAN cameras of his meeting with Ukrainian President Petro Poroshenko in March 2016 where he threatened to terminate $1 billion in U.S. aid if the prosecutor that was investigating Burisma wasn't fired within six-hours.

It becomes even more interesting when we consider that Nancy Pelosi was actively engaged in impeachment activities designed to both cover for Biden and keep those presidential candidates serving in the Senate from campaigning against Biden just as the primary caucus and primary process was about to begin.

Obviously, since the Impeachment rests on the idea that Trump was attacking a political opponent, it falls upon Schiff and Pelosi to ensure that Biden becomes the Democratic nominee. As known from the timeline, on the date of the Ukraine call in which a request for any documents or information related to the Bidens was made, Joe Biden could only "hope" he would not repeat his previous failed attempts to gain a Presidential nomination.

Realistically, there was only a minor chance or probability of his being the nominee – as Bernie Sanders would emphasize, Biden's record is one of poor judgment and decisions combined with support for anti-social policies.

The Biden defenders attack the prosecutor, but as John Solomon wrote on 6 November 2019 and confirmed by documents he obtained through the Freedom of Information Act (FOIA) which all fit perfectly in the timeline:

> *"That became poignantly public when Biden leveraged the threat of canceling $1 billion in U.S. aid in March 2016 to get Ukraine to fire its top prosecutor, Viktor Shokin, who just happened to oversee the Burisma probe. A month before the firing, Shokin escalated the corruption probe against Burisma by seizing the company owner's property and assets.*
>
> *Shokin says he was making plans to interview Hunter Biden and insists he was fired because he refused to stand down on the Burisma probe. Joe Biden insists he prompted Shokin's firing because he believed the prosecutor was ineffective."*

Was Biden asserting a State Department falsehood structured within a scenario created lawyers representing Burisma – a firm that was paying Hunter Biden to do nothing but provide his family name?

On 14 January 2020, we saw CNN allege a statement by Bernie

Sanders made to Elizabeth Warren which asserted that Bernie did not believe a woman could win the Oval. The alleged comment was in a one-on-one meeting – meaning only those two knew the factual basis and any context.

Effectively echoing a view that would apply to the House impeachment hearings, Sanders said:

> *"It's sad that, three weeks before the Iowa caucus and <u>a year after that private conversation, staff who weren't in the room are lying about what happened</u>. Do I believe a woman can win in 2020? Of course! After all, Hillary Clinton beat Donald Trump by three million votes in 2016."*

Of course, the fake news is made interesting by the fact that, in 2015, when there was a movement to get Warren to run for President, Sanders supported the possibility: *"I am a great fan of Elizabeth, and as for what people do and why they don't do it, I am not going to speculate."* At the time, that speculation was rather generalized and Warren eventually made the decision not to run in 2016.

But, when the issue was raised on 14 January, the comment by Warren skirted the year-old conversation to be as sharp as Reagan's one on age – the one about him not holding his opponent's youth and inexperience against him – and expressed the success of females. In a different setting, Warren had pointed out she would be *"the youngest woman ever elected"* POTUS.

Sanders finished his response by pointing out that: *"Hillary Clinton won the popular vote by 3 million votes. How could anybody in a million years not believe that a woman could become president of the United States? And let me be very clear. If any of the women on this stage or any of the men on this stage win the nomination, I hope that's not the case, I hope it's me."*

We were witnessing fake news intended to undermine Warren and Sanders while, by default, boosting Biden.

Turning back to the Biden era and boast, another mention in the Ukraine call cam into play the same day House Speaker Pelosi announced who would be here Prosecution Managers – Ambassador to Ukraine Marie Yovanovitch. In 2019, Ukrainian Prosecutor General Yuriy Lutsenko had told John Solomon that during their first meeting US ambassador Yovanovitch had given him a *"do not prosecute list."*

Specifically, he said: *"Unfortunately, from the first meeting with the U.S. ambassador in Kyiv, [Yovanovitch] gave me a list of people whom we should not prosecute. My response to that is it is inadmissible. Nobody in this country, neither our president nor our parliament nor our ambassador, will stop me from prosecuting whether there is a crime."* But, of course, Yovanovitch worked for the State Department and its boss had been lobbied by Burisma with the name dropping and influence of the Bidens.

There was also mention of the embezzlement 4.4 million dollars in U.S. government technical assistance which had gone missing and was believed to have been embezzled, but Lutsenko related: *"we got the letter from the U.S. Embassy, from the ambassador, that the money that we are speaking about [was] under full control of the U.S. Embassy, and that the U.S. Embassy did not require our legal assessment of these facts. The situation was actually rather strange because the funds we are talking about were designated for the prosecutor general's office also and we told [them] we have never seen those, and the U.S. Embassy replied there was no problem."*

Curiously, apparently, those funds never appeared and the Ambassador who said *"there was no problem"* would later claim both Prosecutor Shokin and Prosecutor Lutsenko were not to be trusted – but she was recalled by the Trump administration.

Rudy Giuliani, himself a former prosecutor, told the New Yorker, *"I believed that I needed Yovanovitch out of the way. She was going to make the investigations difficult for everybody."* This seems to go with a "Do NOT Prosecute" list that included Burisma and a missing $4million.

On 15 January, we learned of the new documents being added to the Impeachment file before it was to be forwarded to the Senate. Among documents was one suggesting then-Ambassador to Ukraine Marie Yovanovitch was placed under surveillance.

Bernie Sanders took a position Yovanovitch had absolutely done nothing wrong in her role as Ambassador and tweeted: *"It is outrageous that the President's personal lawyers appear to have directed the surveillance of a U.S. ambassador. This must be fully investigated as the Senate conducts the impeachment trial. We have a responsibility to hold this lawless administration to account."*

Yovanovitch's attorney, Lawrence Robbins, issued a statement: *"Needless to say, the notion that American citizens and others were monitoring Ambassador Yovanovitch's movements for unknown purposes is disturbing. We trust that the appropriate authorities will conduct an investigation to determine what happened."*

But would that investigation go back to 2014 and come forward to explain the missing $4million? Or would it just toss dust in the air during the impeachment and serve to extend it past Super Tuesday?

Adding to the dust, the House decided to add the newly court released Parnas documents to the transmitted Impeachment Articles – documents they had not even had time to properly review. This has significance because they were generated by Lev Parnas, who was associated with Rudy Giuliani and relate to Ukraine discussions.

Maine Senator Sue Collins again showed her rational bias when she pondered: "*I wonder why the House did not put that into the record and it's only now being revealed.*" When reminded that Parnas had only just relinquished the evidence, Collins asked, *"Doesn't that suggest that the House did an incomplete job, then?"*

Of course, they were incompetent, Pelosi holding the Articles for 30-days showed there was no real rush and the House, in the interest of both "Due Process" and prosecutorial investigative competence had a just reason to delay. But they preferred to do an "*an incomplete job*" and have, as McConnell pointed out, determined the Senate should do their work for them – again, because they are too incompetent and, it seems, dishonest to fulfill their Constitutional duties properly.

The Democratic National Committee Twitter feed – DNC War Room – said, "*The House subpoenaed these documents way back in October. They were turned over this week because the judge in Parnas's criminal case only just cleared him to do so. Susan Collins is falling in line behind Mitch McConnell, as usual, and engaging in Trump's cover-up.*" Incompetence and impatience are a DNC excuse for the House rushing matters rather than gather the documentary evidence Schiff would then say is the only reliable evidence – evidence he couldn't be bothered to gather throughout his House hearings.

But that matter went to trial with Schiff in charge and doing his prosecutorial lies, misrepresent, and prove himself incompetent as he does "*an incomplete job,*" to be continued after Trump is inaugurated in January 2021. But, he did successfully distract from the pandemic.

On 31 December 2019, weeks after Taiwan had informed WHO China informed WHO of 27 cases of Covid-19 in Wuhan; 9-days later it was reported on Chinese TV. On the 15th, two days before airport screening started, a Washington state resident returning from Wuhan, became the first recorded domestic case; a 2nd case had returned on the 13th and became ill a few days later. On 17 January, CDC and Homeland Security began screening all travelers from Wuhan.

Comprehending the scale of the problem, Intelligence officials understood warned Trump and the House Intelligence Committee – on Tuesday the 21st, America had its first death – it was overshadowed by Senate floor media coverage of Democratic House managers going toe-to-toe with the President's defense team over the need to call the witnesses the House had failed to call in its rush to indict Trump.

The argument over House investigative incompetence became front-page news and a significant distraction from a more important real-world event which, within nine weeks, would alter American lives and work habits. It would create a meaning of life *existential crisis* of a type that would see House and Senate Democrats place their political agenda before the Progress ideals of health and economic welfare that were hallmarks of the Sanders, Warren, and Gabbard campaigns.

Climate Change is *"an existential threat to civilization"*; some said *"re-election of Donald Trump would pose an existential threat to the U.S."*; in 2016, Trump had claimed, *"Our campaign represents a true existential threat like they haven't seen before."*

He warned, in a way proved true by a special interest agenda provisions Schumer and Pelosi inserted into the March economic stimulus package: *"There is nothing the political establishment will not do — no lie that they won't tell, to hold their prestige and power at your expense."*

Nancy Pelosi had said the impeachment was urgent, but she did not hesitate to delay transmission of the Articles until Covid-19 was determined to be a Novel Coronavirus – continuing that delay until America had seen its first death. Then, 2-months later, when "social distancing" had entered the behavioral lexicon, she would suddenly object to bipartisan legislation intended to mitigate economic effects resulting from efforts to stop transmission of the *Wuhan* or *Chinese virus*.

"Coincidence," in a political context, can be rather interesting – especially when it accompanies an effort to fabricate a justification to remove the President during a global pandemic.

CHAPTER TWO – BIDEN HOAX

"While we celebrated the birth of Jesus Christ, the Prince of Peace, Congress & Trump passed a $738B war budget, instead of providing for the health, safety, prosperity & well-being of the American people & our planet. Stand with me to end this insanity"
~ Representative Tulsi Gabbard, Xmas 2019

Major Premise: If the president commits a criminal act, then he can be impeached.

Minor Premise: The president does not commit a criminal act.

Conclusion: Therefore, the president cannot be impeached.

Is this a valid or an invalid argument?

Curious dichotomy – Impeachment versus High Crime. Or, as we have seen with Trump, House Action versus Senate/legal Reality.

Both "crime" and "misdemeanor" are statutory criminal acts. High ones require there to be something of a criminal status to justify a conviction. Legal experts agree, there does not need to be a crime for the House to impeach. Impeach can be, as it has been (with exception of Nixon) political act...even Clinton was political — revolving around broad or narrow definition of *"sexual relations."* A definition that can range from *"being alone with"* to *"having intercourse."*

But a statutory violation is needed for conviction — the second half of impeachment. An analogy would be running for President, being a candidate, if you are 30 years old or not a natural-born citizen. It's perfectly legal to run. But you cannot be elected and sworn in — because you don't meet eligibility standards. The CRIMINAL ACT is the Senate eligibility standard, which is why the Articles are a sham.

Sitting through the winter break, awaiting the passing of the impeachment papers to the Senate, it has yet to dawn on the masses enraptured by beauty and mystery of The Emperor's New Clothes that they are fighting to make Mike Pence – a non-POTUS COUSIN – the President.

It is an act of shattering historic tradition that allows Pence to occupy the Oval for a year or as much as nine years. That is, from whenever Trump is convicted of a "HIGH CRIME" for flagging Biden in Ukraine corruption investigation findings so they can be sent to the Attorney General for a determination if they support Biden's public confession where he asserted:

"And I went over, I guess, the 12th, 13th time to Kyiv. And I was supposed to announce that there was <u>another</u> billion-dollar loan guarantee. ... I had gotten a commitment from Poroshenko and from Yatsenyuk that they would take action against the state prosecutor. And they didn't.

"So they said they had — they were walking out to a press conference. I said, nah, I'm not going to — or, we're not going to give you the billion dollars. They said, you have no authority. You're not the president. The president said — I said, call him. I said, I'm telling you, you're not getting the billion dollars. I said, you're not getting the billion. I'm going to be leaving here in, I think it was about six hours. I looked at them and said: I'm leaving in six hours. If the prosecutor is not fired, you're not getting the money. Well, son of a bitch. (Laughter.)

He got fired. And they put in place someone who was solid at the time."

The C-SPAN video of the Biden confession was accompanied by a caption: *"Former Vice President Joe Biden confesses to being in charge of Ukraine for the Obama Administration, and withholding $1 billion in loan guarantees from the USA to force Ukraine to fire prosecutor who was looking into the company that Hunter Biden was receiving $83,000+ PER MONTH from"*

So it was C-SPAN that made the connection between Hunter Biden Burisma and Vice President Joe Biden's act of extortion – which he indicated was approved by President Barack Obama. That would mean Obama was also guilty of any crimes associated with the act.

In terms of Federal Law, Biden declared he and Obama had the authority to terminate the $1 billion in appropriated loan guarantees – and authority that *The Impoundment Control Act of 1974* states is reserved for Congress. The President can delay money for 45 Session Days, while Congress considers changes to the appropriation unless the expiration day is reached within that period – which means the money must be released.

To assert a violation by President Trump, Congress would need to establish the funds were held beyond 45 Congressional session days without the involvement of Congress. The timeline burden of proof would be daunting – well beyond anything the House committee had done to gather real evidence, as opposed to hearsay and supposition.

Consider ARTICLE I: ABUSE OF POWER.

What does "Abuse of Power" really mean? The Article says:

"Using the powers of his high office, President Trump solicited the interference of a foreign government, Ukraine, in the 2020 United States Presidential election."

Because they specified Ukraine and 2020 elections, the context and specificity become a factor. Is Ukraine's corruption related to the election? Is it more involved than a record economic expansion, low unemployment, the USMCA trade agreement, or an agreement with China for the purchase of billions of dollars in American agricultural products?

What did Trump *"solicit"*? It all goes to the Ukraine phone call which, on 24 September 2019, Representative Mark Meadows initially characterized with the words: *"So we are all clear what's happening: House Democrats are supposedly beginning an impeachment inquiry, and building it on an anonymous secondhand complaint they haven't seen... which describes a call transcript that they haven't read."*

Since we now have a transcript, rather than Rep. Adam Schiff's invented and dishonest version, we that Trump was the one to assert influence: *"President Zelenskyy: Well yes, to tell you the truth, we are trying to work hard because we wanted to drain the swamp here in our country. We brought in many many new people. Not the old politicians, not the typical politicians, because we want to have a new format and a new type of government. You are a great teacher for us and in that."*

We then see numerous paragraphs of Zelenskyy praising Trump and American, followed by Trump saying: *"I would like you to do us a favor though because our country has been through a lot and Ukraine knows a lot about it. I would like you to find out what happened with this whole situation with Ukraine,..."* He then has a sentence that trips over connections before indirectly invokes the 1998/9 corruption investigation treaty by saying, *"There are a lot of things that went on, the whole situation. I think you're surrounding yourself with some of the same people. I would like to have the Attorney General call you or your people and I would like you to get to the bottom of it."*

The "*drain the swamp*" provides the basis for understanding "*the same people*" reference.

The "*Attorney General*" references the structure established in the 1998 treaty. We see references to *Crowdstrike* – which would be CrowdStrike Holdings, Inc., a cybersecurity technology firm based in Sunnyvale, California which has been associated with false conspiracy theories. In 2016, the Democratic National Committee paid them to investigate a hack of its server, which it determined emanated from Russia or Russians working from Ukraine as part of the Russian cyber propaganda operation which had proved successful in its Georgia and Crimea operations.

It shouldn't be hard for those interested in the logic behind creating possible and known Ukraine connections to research them. But, there are a wealth of general and specific papers on the Russian cyber propaganda operations – here is a sample of three rather diverse choices: "Ukraine: Russia's New Art of War", by Ioana-Nelia Bercean; "NATO's Response to Hybrid Threats" ISBN: 978-88-96898-12-3; "Towards a Disinformation Resilient Society? The Experience of the Czech Republic", Cosmopolitan Civil Societies: an Interdisciplinary Journal, Vol. 11, No. 1, 2019.

Of course, there are analysis reports like "Russian Digital Media and Information Ecosystem in Turkey" {2019, EDAM Policy Reports}: "*In recent years, Russian digital information operations, including disinformation, fake news, and election meddling have assumed prominence in international news and scholarly research outlets.*"

Those who prefer to be ignorant of the scope of the established Russian operations in cyber warfare will disavow the Russian skills in propaganda systems as affirmed in CIA reports since the 1960s. They are the same class of individuals who deny climate change, bought into the "Obama was born in Kenya" Birther theories or, in classic times, had described the wondrous beauty of *The Emperor's New Clothes*.

In October 2019, it was reported that a new survey found more than 45% of Americans believe that demons and ghosts are real. The question asked was basic: "*Generally speaking, do you believe that each of the following do or do not exist?*" The four choices they had were: demons, ghosts, vampires and other supernatural beings.

Consider that 22 percent said demons "definitely exist," and 20 percent said ghosts "definitely exist." Step it down and 24 percent said demons "probably exist" and 25 percent said ghosts "probably exist."

Now consider that one-in-eight believe that Vampires are real. With those numbers comprising your base demographic, its easy to say *"Climate Change is a Chinese Hoax."* It's also easy to say *"President Trump is a Crook."* Or to recite a false transcript or a phone call and have it quoted, even when the real transcript is made public.

In the Ukraine phone call, Trump did say, *"The other thing, There's a lot of talk [C-SPAN] about Biden's son, that Biden stopped the prosecution and a lot of people want to find out about that so whatever you can do with the Attorney General would be great. Biden went around bragging that he stopped the prosecution so if you can look into it ... It sounds horrible to me."*

What sounds horrible to Trump or anyone realizing Biden was bragging of committing extortion of a foreign government using a Congressional appropriation, is not horrible to Impeachment crazed Swamp Denizens in the House of Representatives or Senate.

That lack of horror is made all the worse by the fact that Nadler and Schiff both defined their *"quid pro quo"* as perfectly conforming to that exact extortion/bribery/coercion model – an explicit violation of 18 U.S.C. and other long-standing Federal statutes.

A few days after Xmas, Alan Dershowitz wrote an analysis of the legal ramifications on the Impeachment after Joe Biden stated he would refuse to obey a Senate Subpoena, then backpedaled to clarify his statement to require a legally justified court order.

Dershowitz stated:

"Biden has now taken the legs out from under the second article of impeachment voted on by the House against President Trump.

"That article accuses the president of "obstruction of Congress" for doing essentially what Biden said he would do, namely demanding a court order before he would comply with what he believes to be partisan subpoenas issued by one chamber of Congress.

"Put another way, by echoing Trump, Biden has provided the president with an airtight defense to the second article.

"The clear implication of this clarification is that Biden would not comply with a subpoena that has "no legal basis" unless the courts compel him to do so.

"Ironically, the original statement that Biden made about not complying, even when taken with his clarification, may now give

the Trump legal team a more compelling basis for calling the former vice president as a witness. He could be asked to justify his original refusal to comply with a Senate subpoena, and then be asked why the refusal by Trump is any more obstructive than his."

On the same day as the Dershowitz article, Tulsi Gabbard was quoted saying, *"I think impeachment, unfortunately, will only further embolden Donald Trump, increase his support and the likelihood that he'll have a better shot at getting elected while also seeing the likelihood that the House will lose a lot of seats to Republicans."*

But then, Congressman Steve Scalise was also accusing House Speaker Nancy Pelosi of attempting an impeachment 'quid pro quo' by threatening to delay both the transmission of Articles of Impeachment and the required appointment of "managers" (prosecutors).

During a televised interview, Scalise said:

"The House broke a lot of rules to ram through this impeachment charade...The Senate will hold a fair trial, you'll see an acquittal, everybody knows it will end in acquittal.

"You can't have it both ways, I think people see through this charade, it's a political charade. It's not what our founders intended impeachment to be used for...there was no crime committed and so now all they're doing is trying to attack the president personally because their field is so weak on the Democratic side."

Phrased another way, Speaker Pelosi was using impeachment to manipulate the 2020 election – she was *"in fact"* doing exactly what she, Schiff, and Nadler were accusing Trump of doing *"in theory."*

The theory of *"solicited interference'* would only be valid if it could be established that Joseph Biden would be the actual nominee for the Democrats. But he had gone for that role three times and failed against individuals with far less public recognition and broad-based support than either Elizabeth Warren or Bernie Sanders.

Biden has a long history of having his ethics questioned; *"The Senator from MBNA"* was a nickname he earned by pushing laws that favored them. In 2008, CBS News reported that both Joe and his son Hunter Biden were receiving "consulting fees" from MBNA at a time when the *"senator supported legislation that was promoted by the credit card industry and opposed by consumer groups."*

Ten years later, Biden was bragging about using extortion to have a Ukraine Prosecutor General fired, and a firm that might have been under investigation was Burisma – which was paying *"consulting fees"* to a firm associated with Hunter Biden and had made Hunter a Board member, which permitted him to receive a reported $50,000 a month for doing nothing (in addition to what his firm received).

When interviewed by CBS News in October 2019, the 49-year-old Hunter Biden said: *"Did I Make a Mistake? Maybe in the Grand Scheme of Things, Yeah. ...But did I make a mistake based on some ethical lapse? Absolutely not. ...What I regret is not taking into account that there would be a Rudy Giuliani and a president of the United States that would be listening to this – this ridiculous conspiracy idea. I gave a hook to some very unethical people to act in illegal ways to try to do some harm to my father... That's where I made the mistake. So I take full responsibility for that. Did I do anything improper? No, not in any way. Not in any way whatsoever. ...I don't think that there's a lot of things that would have happened in my life if my last name wasn't Biden. Because my dad was Vice President of the United States, there's literally nothing, as a young man or as a full-grown adult that – my father in some way hasn't had influence over."*

The impeachment logic is magnificent: A former Vice President brags of violating multiple Federal Laws; the Congress appropriates money to investigate corruption and a sitting President asks that those conducting the investigation flag certain findings, and if they exist, that they are turned over to the Attorney General. As a result of the flag request, the President is impeached and no data is transferred – the lack of data is then used to justify the impeachment.

It might not be so bad, if the New York Times had not published a story on 8 December 2015 asserting *"the credibility of the vice president's anti-corruption message may have been undermined by the association of his son, Hunter Biden, with one of Ukraine's largest natural gas companies, Burisma Holdings, and with its owner, Mykola Zlochevsky, who was Ukraine's ecology minister under former President Viktor F. Yanukovych before he was forced into exile."*

On 16 January, Sen. Rand Paul (R-KY), stated the obvious.

There is documented connection between Ukrainian corruption and multiple members of the Biden family, and transcript of Trump's call with the Ukrainian President expressed concerns over Joe Biden bragging about using extortion or bribery to manipulate the interior workings of a foreign government.

Rand said *"It goes to the heart of the matter. If the president is being accused of withholding foreign aid, and his argument is, 'Well, we were studying corruption, and we wanted to know about corruption in Ukraine,' and I think the Bidens are as corrupt as the day is long. No young man who is the son of a politician gets $50,000 a month who has no experience, working for a Ukrainian oligarch. You know, for goodness sakes — it smells to high heaven. It smells like corruption. And every day on the mainstream media, they say, 'Oh, there's no 'there' there. This has been investigated. There is no corruption.' I think the American people don't buy it. Here's the thing: Fair is fair. If they're going to put the president through this, they're going to have to have witnesses on both sides."*

What Rand didn't mention was the pattern of profiteering that extended to Biden's younger brother Frank Biden has been capitalizing on the name since before Biden became Vice President in 2009.

When interviewed, like Hunter, Frank was very candid about it and said his last name *"a tremendous asset"* because of the family's record of *"taking help care of people who need,"* of the kind which brought those contract profits via government approvals of the kind he obtained for the for-profit *Mavericks in Education* charter schools.

As a longtime Florida real estate developer, Frank Biden has leveraged the Biden name in the same way Hunter described when he was interviewed and said everything he had came from the name. In Frank's case, over the years, leveraged his famous last name and prominent Washington connections to help land charter school contracts from local Florida officials, and, as reported by ABC News, his compensation was $70,000 per year for a five-year period which, coincidentally, ended around 2014.

Three years later, in 2012, a whistleblower lawsuit alleged that the Palm Beach Maverick school altering student enrollment records to secure more government funding, two years after that, in 2014, two Pinellas County school district executives filed a lawsuit naming Frank Biden as a defendant in a case which accused Mavericks of *"falsely inflating the operating expenses associated with the operations of the charter schools"* to divert $22 million in *"funds from the education of the students to the owners of [Mavericks]."*

Audits covering those same years for *Maverick's* schools in Palm Beach and Broward Counties affirmed the issues and appropriate "action plans" were instituted, while the 2012 case was resolved by a confidential settlement and the 2014 case was dropped. The schools' below-par performance continued until 2017 when *EdisonLearning* purchased them from *Maverick*.

In September 2019, Joe Biden made this statement distancing himself from the family use of his name or contacts, claiming: "*I have never discussed with my son or my brother or anyone else anything having to do with their businesses, period.*"

A month before Biden used extortion against Ukraine, we find Burisma's lobbyists, who were recommended by Biden, trying to get Obama's State Department to leverage Hunter Biden to obtain help in the cover-up of corruption at Burisma. An email dated 24 February 2016 makes it clear Blue Star Strategies was pushing the idea Burisma was not corrupt and echoed the propaganda pitch given the British.

The comical aspect is the memo asserts things we now hear being asserted by Trump's team – no due process, no consideration of exculpatory evidence, and no rational basis for the US Government's "*determination that the company is corrupt*" or in Trump's case no statutory justification to assert a "High Crime" has been committed. With Trump, we citation of a statutory violation; with Burisma there is a paper trail and convictions, with more charges pending the arrest of *Zlochevsky* – assuming his whereabouts can be determined.

It is known that Hunter Biden joined Burisma's board in April 2014; this was about two months after British authorities requested information from Ukraine, just as Trump would in 2019 – the British were interested in the money laundering by Burisma Holdings and its owner Zlochevsky – Ukraine's minister of environmental protection under then-President Viktor Yanukovych, who, on 22 February, fled to Russia in the aftermath of the "*Revolution of Dignity*".

The violence and threat to the president was an outgrowth of Euromaidan ('European Square') movement which had begun, on 21 November 2013, with public protests in Kiev's Independence Square (Maidan Nezalezhnosti) with complaints of human rights violations and the catch-all "*abuse of power*".

Later, when speaking before the Odesa Financial Forum on 24 September 2015, US Ambassador Geoffrey Pyatt would say:

"During my tenure as U.S. ambassador to Ukraine, I have been inspired by the Ukrainian people's demand for accountability. During the Revolution of Dignity, and every day since, Ukrainians have persevered, often at great personal cost, in order to determine their own future.

"And Ukraine's leaders are listening. Despite an invader in the east – using weapons and words to weaken, dispirit, and distract – national, regional, and local officials are moving forward with difficult political and economic reforms to bring Ukraine closer to its chosen European future."

Pyatt went on to describe American efforts to help create an honest Prosecution and investigation system and then asserted this:

"That obstacle is the failure of the institution of the Prosecutor General of Ukraine to successfully fight internal corruption. Rather than supporting Ukraine's reforms and working to root out corruption, corrupt actors within the Prosecutor General's office are making things worse by openly and aggressively undermining reform."

He then references a British case against the owner of Burisma:

"For example, in the case of former Ecology Minister Mykola Zlochevsky, the U.K. authorities had seized 23 million dollars in illicit assets that belonged to the Ukrainian people. Officials at the PGO's office were asked by the U.K to send documents supporting the seizure.

"Instead they sent letters to Zlochevsky's attorneys attesting that there was no case against him. As a result, the money was freed by the U.K. court and shortly thereafter the money was moved to Cyprus.

"The misconduct by the PGO officials who wrote those letters should be investigated, and those responsible for subverting the case by authorizing those letters should – at a minimum – be summarily terminated.

"Even as we support the work of the new Anti-Corruption Commission, and the recruitment of new prosecutors, we have urged Prosecutor General Shokin to empower Deputy Prosecutors Sakvarelidze and Kasko to implement reforms and bring to justice those who have violated the law, regardless of rank or status. We are prepared to partner with reformers within the PGO in the fight for anti-corruption."

You should note that Shokin is cited in the context of being part of the solution and not the problem. And we already have a timeline that shows *"Zlochevsky's attorneys"* included members of the Biden family lobbying the State Department to facilitate the acceptance of letters *"attesting that there was no case against him."* Even during the impeachment process, with opening arguments about to be made on the Senate floor, there are still people arguing that Burisma was involved in no wrongdoing – while Zlochevsky is in hiding to escape the overwhelming evidence of the crimes committed through Burisma Holdings.

Pyatt concluded his comments by informing the audience that U.S. Secretary of Commerce Penny Pritzker would return to Ukraine the following month and would be evaluating the progress of reforms and opportunities *"to establish more connections and partnerships with U.S. businesses and investors."*

Pyatt places us in September 2015, while Viktor Shokin became Prosecutor General on 10 February 2015 – 7-months earlier - and Joe Biden boasted of being responsible for his firing in April 2016. Biden's timeline doesn't work, and this is why.

Vitaliy Kasko – Viktor Shokin's deputy overseeing international cooperation and helping in asset-recovery investigations – stated Shokin took no action to pursue cases against Zlochevsky throughout 2015 and claimed he had urged Shokin to pursue the investigations.

But Kasko is on record saying: *"There was no pressure from anyone from the U.S. to close cases against Zlochevsky. It was shelved by Ukrainian prosecutors in 2014 and through 2015."*

Kasko clearly said the problem dated to 2014 – the year before Shokin was hired. In 2019, Shokin testified and stated in a media interview that his predecessor's documentation vanished around the time he was hired and wasn't there to use. This infers the files created under his predecessor, Vitaly Yarema, someone had used a leadership transfer to remove or destroy the "shelved" case file evidence.

Even so, we know Shokin was actively freezing Zlochevsky and Burisma Holdings assets during the same period the Biden name was being invoked to support claims there was no corruption associated with Hunter Biden's employer.

We also know, "Biden backed" pressure was being exerted on Britain and USA with false claims of Zlochevsky innocence reflected in the February 2015-March 2016 push to remove Shokin and replace him with Biden's version of a "solid" prosecutor – one with no legal training, knowledge, or background.

We have Joe Biden's admission of Extortion and bribery, in his own words as captured on video by C-SPAN: "*I'm going to be leaving here, in, I think it was about six hours. I looked at them and said: I'm leaving in six hours. If the prosecutor is not fired, you're not getting the money.*"

Problem is, Biden's brag doesn't fit the timeline, but it does fit the facts in the real timeline – including his criminal involvement.

In 2019 Shokin stated threats made to the Ukraine President were done by telephone and Ukraine transcripts exist. Since Biden would have used an official government phone, there would be records of the calls and, possibly, American recording.

The "*quid pro quo*" bribery and extortion might not have been on a six-hour time clock – more like a four-month period of persistent threats. But imagine how thrilled Nader or Schiff would be if they had Biden's calls or even his C-SPAN confession, with Trump being the one making the very same threats. Would their followers be asserting an "administration policy" defense? Or would we be seeing a valid move to impeach, with a clear likelihood of conviction?

There is no question they would declare it absolutely rock-solid evidence of extortion and bribery; any honest attorney would agree and the Articles of Impeachment would probably have passed with a unanimous bipartisan vote.

Curiously, the only exculpatory thing Biden's brag has going for it is that Shokin submitted a letter of resignation on 16 February 2016, but Ukraine authorities reinstated him on 16 March 2016, only to find a need to have him formally dismissed by a parliamentary vote on 29 March 2016.

However, while he made six Ukraine trips as Vice President, not one was during the period between February and March 2016, or even during the whole 2016-year. The six documented Ukraine trips were: 1. July 20-22, 2009; 2. April 21-22, 2014; 3. June 6, 2014; 4. Nov. 20-21, 2014; 5. Dec. 7-8, 2015; 6. Jan. 16-17, 2017.

Curiously, Biden's boast included a statement about how many trips he had made to Kiev (more than twice the official count):

"And I went over, I guess, the 12th, 13th time to Kiev. And I was supposed to announce that there was another billion-dollar loan

guarantee. And I had gotten a commitment from Poroshenko and from Yatsenyuk that they would take action against the state prosecutor. And they didn't."

The first Billion dollars was appropriated in March 2014 as part of a $27 Billion International Monetary Fund financing package and done in conjunction with the European Union. As a loan guarantee program, this included energy assistance designed to counter Russia's announcement it was ending Ukraine's national gas supply discounts and that would explain the contact between Joe Biden and Burisma – a natural gas firm. That contact would have brought Hunter and his partner to the attention of Burisma founder Mykola Zlochevsky.

From 27 February 2014 until 14 April 2016, Arseniy Yatsenuk was Ukraine Prime Minister and in April 2017 was temporarily placed on the Interpol's international wanted list for violation of three articles of the Criminal Code of Russia – including murder; however, since Russia's request did not conform Article 3 of Interpol constitution, it was dismissed. From 7 June 2014 to 20 May 2019, Petro Poroshenko was President of Ukraine; in April 2019 he was succeeded by President Volodymyr Zelensky, who was on the call with President Trump.

During Biden's first visit he met with Prime Minister Arseniy Yatsenyuk on 22 April 2014 and was there during the "Revolution for Dignity"; as we see, three of his visits and the payment to Hunter's firm Rosemont Seneca Bohai coincided with the period Kasko stated the investigations into Burisma halted.

Setting aside Biden's inability to know how many trips he made to Ukraine if we look at date #2, we see Biden would have met with Yatsenuk and acting President Oleksandr Turchynov – both their predecessors having been removed by Ukraine Parliament in February 2014, and concurrent to the Russian Annexation of Crimea on 22–23 February 2014. The annexation resulted in the first aid bill H.R.4278 – Ukraine Support Act.

Note a coincidence with trip two – which coincides with Hunter Biden being hired by Burisma Holdings, and raises the question as to whether he was on Air force Two or why Burisma would hire him just when his father goes to Ukraine. We do know this was also the time when the twice-monthly "consulting services" payments of $83,333 to Rosemont Seneca Bohai LLC, the firm of Hunter Biden and business partner, Devon Archer, began and that they continued for 18 months ending around the time of Joe Biden's fifth visit, his discovery Shokin was honest.

Biden's fifth visit was 7 December 2015; this would have been the only opportunity for him to have personally bribed or extorted Ukraine officials in a manner consistent with his C-SPAN documented bragging. At the time, Shokin had been in office ten months and was actively freezing Burisma assets and preparing indictments – inferring that was the action Joe Biden sought to stop.

Biden's sixth and final Ukraine visit was a stopover on the way to a conference in Switzerland from 15-18 January 2017; Donald John Trump's inauguration was a few days later.

In October 2019, Ukraine's current prosecutor general, Ruslan Ryaboshapka, stated his office would revisit about 15 legal cases closed or dormant in recent years, including several involving Burisma and its oligarch Mykola Zlochevsky.

While the timeline conflicts with Biden's bragging, it does match perfectly with the "*consulting*" payments and cessation of the Burisma investigations before Viktor Shokin's appointment. Based on the documented dates Biden was in Ukraine, and interview statements by Shokin, the extortion treats Biden had admitted to were being delivered by telephone. It is believed the calls were made between 12 and 19 February; that would mean a Federal call record, which might have been recorded as an archival record and carry the importance of the Nixon Tape Recordings.

The Foreign Corrupt Practices Act (15 USC 78dd-1) of 1977 is a law that criminalizes foreign bribery and makes it illegal for a U.S. person to coerce or influence, through bribery or extortion, a foreign nation into taking action that might financially benefit that person, his family or business. Biden appears to have boasted of violating this act.

Biden stated there was "*another billion-dollar loan guarantee*" – which appears not to have existed since the Trump Administration brought the appropriated funds total to $1.5 Billion. So either Biden is senile or Machiavellian and intentionally distorting reality to cover for the money laundering of corruption funds he arranged to have paid to his son Hunter. Such an act would be consistent with other modes of known family enrichment which began to emerge in media reports during the slow news cycle created by Pelosi holding the Articles of Impeachment.

CHAPTER THREE – GROW UP

"California and New York must do something about their TREMENDOUS Homeless problems. They are setting records!"
~ Trump Tweet, December 2019

Homelessness is highest in New York and California – highest in those districts whose representatives were attacking Trump rather than focusing on helping American Citizens live a better life. In March 2020, America would discover these two locations, which provided the leadership for impeachment attacks, are also the national hotbed for the Wuhan virus and American deaths.

There is also the gerrymandering element mentioned in 'NEXT 2020" (book 7, the previous installment in this series).

Homeless people have something in common with those illegal migrants who take advantage of a lack of a secure border fence or wall of the type advocated by Barack Obama and Donald Trump. In both cases, the bodies count in the census and for legislative representation, but neither can vote and have no real voice. In fact, they tend to be the most silent of people – trees in human bodies.

To some degree, trees have better representation and protection – they have the Environmental Protection Agency.

The Department of Housing and Urban Development (HUD) reported, from 2018 to 2019, homelessness in California increased by 21,306 people or 16.4 percent. The highest homeless populations in the United States are in New York City 76,501, Los Angeles 55,188, Seattle 11,643, Washington D.C. 7,473, San Jose 7,394, San Francisco 6,858, Philadelphia 5,693. Their common factors are Democrats who want to Impeach Trump, residents who voted 80% for Hillary Clinton, and...

At the start of 2020, California had a minimum wage of $13 per hour and New York State mandated $11.80; only Washington D.C. had a minimum wage of $15 – the level Bernie Sanders had advocated and one that approached a rational wage level designed to minimize the welfare supplementation which aided large corporations like Walmart to book additional unearned profits.

If we compare the minimum wage to the homeless, we see that is no correlation. Philadelphia has the Federal minimum wage, while Seattle is $13.50; the highest homeless rates are in California, which is also the state with the most people pushing for impeachment and open borders – those who follow Ronald Reagan's opposition to fences and control of Climate Migrants which will, over the next decade, be the source of population growth overrunning all northern hemisphere nations with people who do not speak the language and have no usable skills.

Globally, before 2050, Climate Migrants are projected to exceed 1.6 Billion people – roughly the 2019 population of China. The United States could see a 20-percent population surge – unless the Wall is in place and a proper screening and relocation process is in place.

Maine's Republican Senator Sue Collins came to office at a time when the Internet was in its infancy and Maine was the first state to provide its public school students with computers. In 2020, the Maine minimum wage was $12.00 per hour – equal to Connecticut and lower than only three states and the District of Columbia.

Collins has also shown exceptionally rational leadership skills, playing dictatorial moderator when Swamp Denizens did their worst and consistently proving victorious.

Vermont's Independent Senator Bernard 'Bernie' Sanders has achieved a status as the longest-serving independent in congressional history and proponent of an above poverty minimum wage where the Federal Government is no longer effectively subsidizing the employer. His state's 2020 minimum wage was $10.96 per hour, indicating his leadership abilities are such that he can't even convince his own state to go to or above $15.

While the Senate was preparing for the Impeachment, Hillary Clinton was interviewed about a Hulu documentary on her career and was asked about an old Bernie Sanders comment she had made: "*He was in Congress for years. He had one senator support him. Nobody likes him, nobody wants to work with him, he got nothing done. He was a career politician. It's all just baloney and I feel so bad that people got sucked into it.*"

She then told the Hollywood Reporter: "*I will say, however, that it's not only him, it's the culture around him. It's his leadership team. It's his prominent supporters. It's his online Bernie Bros and their relentless attacks on lots of his competitors, particularly the women.*"

Given the Clinton assessment, would Sanders be electable? If he was elected, would he demonstrate leadership characteristics or the fear that can hold politicians and foreign leaders in line?

The immediate backlash over the Hollywood Reporter article triggered a change of tune and invoked the result of Hillary's 'Basket of Deplorables' blunder: *"I thought everyone wanted my authentic, unvarnished views! But, to be serious, the number one priority for our country and world is retiring Trump, and, as I always have, I will do whatever I can to support our nominee."*

Meanwhile, Sanders had to contradict an op-ed penned by one of his supporters postulating the former vice president was corrupt. Sanders stated, *"It is absolutely not my view that Joe is corrupt in any way. And I'm sorry that that op-ed appeared."*

Since Biden is corrupt, saying so can cost you votes – especially when the House is working to cover-up that corruption and impose it on Trump for seeking to investigate Biden's brag about it.

During a WMUR News 9 interview, Tulsi Gabbard addressed the Clinton comment by saying: *"It's time to grow up. This isn't high school. We're talking about real challenges that our country needs to address and the need for real leadership to focus on them, not on what's going on in Washington and the schoolyard cliques or whatever else it may be."*

But because the political establishment behaves like schoolyard brats, throughout the Trump Card series I have referenced Trump and his Queens Schoolyard approach to diplomacy and his political swamp denizen opposition. And inserting it at this point in the chapter broke the flow the way such comments break the political flow – a technique Trump knowingly uses to command and control the media.

Our topic flow was getting into Minimum Wages and the reality that low income hampers economic growth, and the record economic expansion Trump was so proud of was pushing the demographic limits to the point where both Social Security and Minimum Wage revenue would become the dominant influence in its continuation.

Throughout his career, Joe Biden has been a proud deficit hawk who followed a Reagan Republican-style approach that attacked social program expenditures, rather than corrects their source of revenue. In 1994, he said: *"When I argued that we should freeze federal spending, I meant Social Security as well. I meant Medicare and Medicaid. I meant veterans' benefits. I meant every single solitary thing in the government. And I not only tried it once, I tried it twice, I tried it a third time, and I tried it a fourth time."*

On 16 January 2019, Rep. Robert C. Scott [D-VA-3] introduced H.R.582 - Raise the Wage Act, to amend the Fair Labor Standards Act of 1938, and gradually raises the minimum wage to $15 in six annual intervals: $8.40, $9.50, $10.60, $11.70, $12.80, $13.90, and $15.00. The legislation passed 231:199 on Thursday, 18 July 2019, with more Democratic *Noes* that Republican *Ayes*, then forwarded to the Senate.

Concurrent with the House Bill, Sanders introduced the exact same legislation as S.150; it was read twice and then referred to the Committee on Health, Education, Labor, and Pensions – where it died. Had it been acted upon, a $15 wage would be scheduled for 2026 and Bernie Sanders would have been denied a central campaign issue. As is, shows that, after thirty years in the Senate, he still lacks contacts and basic negotiating skills to pass a simple and economically rational piece of legislation.

Worse, the House-Senate Bill starts with a wage lower than the lowest non-federal minimum currently in effect on the State level; the states with higher than federal minimum are already geared toward incremental increases that will keep them higher than any proposed changes.

The current Minimum Wage came into effect on 24 July 2009. In a January campaign speech, Sanders used 1965 as reference saying:

"Four-year public university tuition in 1965 cost $261 a year. Today, it is $10,440 a year. Taxpayers paid for a trillion-dollar bailout to benefit the crooks on Wall Street. I think we can afford to make public colleges tuition-free and cancel all student debt."

In 1965, the baby-boom generation was coming of age; the 26th Amendment would exist until 1 July 1971, when 'coming of age' would drop from twenty-one to eighteen. In 1965, a minimum wage worker received $1.25 per hour – which would be $10.07 in January 2020, or $0.89 less than the Vermont minimum wage. Phrased in terms of purchasing power a single 1965 dollar, could buy what you would need $8.05 to but in January 2020.

If we look at the cost of a gallon of gasoline – even with the wild rate fluctuations over the decades – the price is in line with inflation. In 1965, you could buy three gallons for a dollar; in January 2020, it was as low as $2.215 and as high as $3.662. The inflation calculation ($0.33x8.05) says we could expect what we find a price in the area of $2.66/gallon; allowing for changes and the introduction of biofuels it seems consistent.

Interestingly, in 2007, "experts" were predicting a gallon of gas in 2020 would be $5.00 – so they were significantly wrong. We are also seeing a situation where demographic realities associated with a Baby-Boom followed by a Baby-Bust have caused the Federal Reserve to come to grips with a new reality. It is evident that when handled properly – by someone familiar with finance – demographic changes mean a stable financial system can coexist with low unemployment, low inflation, and low interest rates. This new reality was triggered by the Boomer's turning 70 in 2015 and their Social Security taking on the characteristic of a Universal Basic Income [UBI].

Pending the results of the 2020 census, one-in-five Americans are over the age of 65; one-in-four is under 18; if we factor in all those who are some form of disability, UBI is probably supporting a third of the adult population – though it might be labeled in various ways to be called disability, welfare, survivors benefits, or even unemployment insurance benefits or military and other early retirement pensions.

If we are honest, we realize we have UBI in many forms and it is just a matter of consolidating and dispensing with administrative cost duplications. So long as there are immigrants and non-citizens, we would still need a minimum wage.

Had college costs held to inflation, the tuition cited by Sanders would only be $2,101.05 instead of the $10,440. The cost difference reflects the fact that college costs are non-linear – the introduction of computers or other technological changes and the changes in student population size alter the basic structure defining the public university environment.

In 1965, Baby-Boomers, defined college record enrollments and this meant per student fixed costs were lower; it also meant increased infrastructure expenses which would be spread across several decades; in 2020, maintenance costs related to that infrastructure are being spread across a decreasing enrollment resulting from the Baby-Bust, and that means a higher per-student tuition reflected cost. The rate of inflation is not a valid basis to compare costs.

Sanders is concerned with the combined economic deadening effect of tuition loans expressed in the terms of debt burden on those whose educations will ultimately enrich society.

Those familiar with the Old Testament and the creation of the Tribes are aware that there were twin tribes – the Issachar scholars and Zebulun merchants charged with supporting scholars and their families. There is a rational reason for Capitalists to support Scholars – capitalism sells the product of creative scholarship.

Finding a way to offset the cost of tuition benefits the nation.

Sanders makes a fiscal mistake in asserting he wants to zero out the debt – simply erase or write it off $1.5 trillion in student loan debt associated with 44.7 million borrowers. While it sounds good, writing off the debt would be similar in effect to canceling all credit cards and auto loans, or most mortgage debt.

It sounds really good, but actually has the effect of removing its interest income (4.75% to 15.14%) from the economy. That equates to between $71 and $771 Billion annually; Trump cheered his *Phase One* China agreement bring in $50 Billion in agricultural sales, and Bernie is throwing away 1.5 to 10 times that amount annually.

In the context of Student Loan Debt, Sanders is not addressing real economics. His model is designed to crash the economy at a time when there is a need to modify traditional economic models rather than engage in economic throw-away programs. As is, if the loan debt is not paid the economy will crash; at the same time, the Baby-Bust creates a demographic basis for education cost growth that exceeds the general rate of inflation. As with the National Debt, the model that gave rise to Reaganomics – with debt being paid through Monetization or devaluation of the currency – is what created the situation.

Standard economic theory demands that these economic forces create conflicts and that low unemployment should trigger the higher inflation that was the basis for Reaganomics and the assumption that the National Debt would be handled through Monetization. Of course, Reagan came from an era where mortgage interest rates were 8% and an average yearly inflation rate was 4.06% – a post-World War Two norm until 2009 when it fell to an average of 1.57%. When Reagan was elected in 1980, inflation was 13.5%, while it averaged 9.39% from 1977 to 1981 – a period when the Baby-Boomers were raising their families, buying or renovating homes, and the Co-op/Condo craze was starting.

Reaganomics was predicated on inflation periodically going to double the interest rate in a way that would have the purchasing value of repaid money being at least half that of the borrowed capital. Because that hasn't happened, we are faced with a National Debt Crisis when the Boomer-Bust demographic hits the year 2030.

In January 2020, Kansas City Fed President Esther George saw it "a reset" defining a new world of economics. As stated in the CNBC interview in August 2019: "*With this very low unemployment rate, with wages rising, with the inflation rate staying close to the Fed's target, I think we're in a good place relative to the mandates that we're asked to achieve.*"

At the time, the US-China trade war was affecting the economic growth in both countries but not as much as the economic activity of other nations, and she was concerned with the country falling into the cyclical 11-year recession pattern which the Trump policies have since proved have other causes.

At the time, George observed, "*As you look at global growth weakening and as you look at the amount of uncertainty associated with some of these trade issues, I think both of those are weighing on the outlook. Whether they spill over in a way that we see in the real economy is what I'm watching for.*" While she had been pushing for rate hikes that Trump opposed, the fact George was willing to wait to see how things played out "*in the real economy*" stopped the mistake that might have triggered a recession.

So it was, on 15 January – as the House voted the Impeachment process into the Senate – The Wall Street Journal reported George saying, "*I continue to see the expansion supported by solid growth in consumer spending, with continued weakness in manufacturing and business spending.*"

Naturally, in the context of the population demographics, the idea of people buying, while production capacity relative to population growth had maxed-out, made perfect sense. And a few days later the nation saw the signing of the Phase One Trade Agreement combined with the formalization of USMCA and it became reasonable to assume the "*continued weakness in manufacturing and business spending*" was a forerunner to a restructuring necessary to accommodate the new realities of a century that will be defined both by Global Warming and the shift of populations caused by Climate Change Refugee migration.

On 21 January, day-one of the Senate Impeachment process, Trump was cheering the economy at a conference in Switzerland.

Back in Washington, the Democratic managers were seeking "all documents, communications, and other records" Ukraine related – a process that could take days, weeks, or even months. Reasonably, it would include any and all the Biden related information explored in the previous chapter; that means Biden would be a witness needed to explain his obvious lies.

It also means caucus and primary voters might need to decide if the House Managers are incompetent or if they intended to expose Biden as the liar the timeline shows him to have been when he openly confessed to extortion before the C-SPAN cameras.

Is it possible Schiff and company wanted to do the investigation needed to provide the American side of the Biden data Trump wanted to have flagged by Ukraine?

It didn't really matter. Bernie Sanders said: "*My focus is going to be on impeachment.*" And he and his supporters were determined to keep working "*to defeat the most dangerous president in American history.*" So it was clear he wouldn't mind losing the nomination to a man who boasted of committing extortion and bribery – even if that admission was a braggadocious lie to cover or distract from the money laundering timeline associated with his son Hunter receiving "services rendered" payments.

Trump was in Switzerland with Greta Thunberg and others he dismissed as "*perennial prophets of doom*" on climate change at the annual meeting of the 50th World Economic Forum. But he also said the U.S. would join an initiative to plant a trillion trees and also gave the message "*To every business looking for a place to succeed... there is no better place than the U.S..*"

Trump also said, "*I'm a very big believer in the environment. I want the cleanest water and the cleanest air.*" If he were to achieve it, his place in the environmental corner of history would be as secure as that of Greta Thunberg's family.

Of course, Thunberg responded by denouncing "*empty words and promises*" from world leaders who she belittled by reminding them: "*You say children shouldn't worry ... don't be so pessimistic and then, nothing, silence.*"

For all his talk about Climate Change and rejection of USMCA, because it failed to mention the Climate issue, Senator Sanders never deals with the demographics that have created the problem that was first defined in 1893, when Laureate Svante Arrhenius – awarded the 1903 Nobel Prize for unrelated work in chemistry – associated the end of the ice age with increases in atmospheric carbon dioxide as defined in a formula he devised in 1889 to help quantify those CO_2 emission increases from the then-new reliance on fossil-fuels and various other combustion processes which we now associate with increased global temperatures and the related melting of the polar ice caps.

What is termed the "Greenhouse Effect" was already old when Arrhenius created his equation – it dates back to at least to 1824 when the French mathematician Joseph Fourier realized Earth's atmosphere functioned similarly to a "hotbox" – a wooden box with a glass lid – as devised by Swiss physicist Horace Bénédict de Saussure in the period of the American revolution.

Of curious interest is the fact Arrhenius is an ancestral cousin to Greta Thunberg, the young climate activist who gained sufficient stature to be called to address the United Nations, where she blamed them and the leaders of the Industrial Nations, for threatening the future of all in her generation.

Also of interest is the fact increased global population created the linear connection to Climate Change as predicted by the Arrhenius Equation. And since his prediction, that global population has grown four-times-over, with the biggest expansion beginning in 1945 – now known as the Baby-Boom, that lasted for twenty years.

The combination of the aging Baby-Boomers and a subsequent Baby-Bust defining the period in which their grandchildren or great-grandchildren should have been born, things are coming together to make 2050 the time when science reports global warming had melted glaciers to the point where sea-level rise had maximized. At that point, technological changes like low energy computers, cellphones, and reduced demand for heat in homes will have changed fossil fuel needs; if we toss in local solar, piezoelectric highways, and wireless charging based on ambient electric waves, the Arrhenius Equation infers a stabilization of climate that will take two generations and then last for well over a century.

Senator Sanders and climate activists who focus on fossil fuels or "climate gases" should be focused on those technologies which will spread the way cellphones and laptop computing has. When Sanders invokes 1965, he is looking back to the time when the last of the Baby-Boomers was born and the first of them was graduating college. The purchasing power of $100 in 1965 equaled $805.75 in 2019. During the Carter Administration, double-digit inflation defined the economy – it began with the 1965 increase in inflation caused by Baby-Boomer demand exceeding traditional supply to yield a 3.87% average annual inflation rate.

Reagan's advisors associated the start of the increased inflation rate pattern with general economic rules for the new technological era; they were actually demographic forces caused by traditional "Supply and Demand" that Esther George reported as a *"growth in consumer spending, with continued weakness in manufacturing"* which we can recognize as the transitioning into a Baby-Bust economy.

Instinctively, both Trump and the Chinese have seen the effect of the Baby-Bust and projected it forward. In China, we see how their traditional centralized government reaction is applied. In the Reagan Era, when the Baby-Boom inflation became the basis for monetization of excessive deficit spending and the resulting National Debt.

China turned to the core problem – the number of babies – and in the same year America elected Ronald Reagan, China instituted its One-Child Policy and thus manufactured a Baby-Bust. As a result, in January 2020, demographers are seeing China's population shrink by 2030 and by 2050 those over the age of 60 would account for a third of the population – which should be the same as in the United States where individuals within the society made the children-free decision – which is actively being opposed by the Far-Right.

The general motivation of the Far-Right is to find an excuse to keep growing the population. A curious reality when we consider the Evangelicals profess a belief in the Bible where Revelation states that in the second millennium after the birth of Jesus – this era – global life is to be reduced by a third. We see it happening with the death of species related to Climate Change, and in the Baby-Bust demographic that will see a third of Americans dead by age 80; for Baby-Boomers populations, this means between 2025 and 2045.

If Gen-X is represented by those born between 1961 and 1981, we have a four-year overlap with the Baby-Boomers which places that overlap in the age 60 group by the 2024 election.

"Millennials" (Gen-Y), are those born between 1981 and 1996; they align well with the Chinese demographic, while Gen-Z is broadly represented by those just old enough to recall the Clinton impeachment over the "Oral in the Oval" based definition of "Sexual Relations" – the last of them concurrent with the birth of the Obama era – so they are those born between 1996 and 2010.

Bernie Sanders is part of a pre-World War "Silent Generation" whose youth was indoctrinated with and defined by the Progressivist movement of Franklin D Roosevelt. And we see this cradle training in

Sanders' platform and social pronouncements. Toss in the fact he was born exactly three months before the horrifying news of Pearl Harbor spread across the nation and we would have him raised in a home where war and Nazi anti-Semitism were the persistent topic shaping his view of the world and mental approach to threatening events.

That might sound strange to some, but they are doubtless unaware of the line: "*Give me a child until he is 7 and I will show you the man.*" It is a line from The Philosophy of Aristotle which, about 1900 years later, was used by Ignatius of Loyola at the time America's colonial ancestors were being born, which was about the time Queen Elisabeth reigned over England, and Michel de Nostredame – known as Nostradamus – was composing his Prophecies or *Centuries*.

We can learn about each candidate by learning about their first seven years of life; obviously, we also learn a lot about ourselves by looking to those early years and the subliminal lessons they implanted.

We might also learn about or have motivational guides for the understanding of those who are opposed to progressive programs and promoting impeachment.

We know Trump is interested in his legacy and the way he will be perceived in history. In a perverse way, the attacks actually help him. They have placed him in a special category that, until 2019, had been reserved for those who violated laws – rather than enforce them.

For both Andrew Johnson and Bill Clinton there was a violated law that applied only because things were manipulated to ensure the violation. With Johnson in was *The Tenure of Office Act* which he vetoed and Congress overrode that veto because it wanted to deny the President control over who was serving in his Cabinet. As most know, Clinton was impeached for perjury stemming from a definition of "Sexual Relations" – generally considered to involve intercourse, but the Republican accuser stretched to mean anything sexual.

With Clinton, another issue came into play – the boundary that exists between an elected individual's Official Office and Personal Life.

Is it legitimate to enquire into the sex-life of an elected official so that you can then entrap them when they seek to keep it private? Having asked, can you then play rhetorical games and use an inclusive definition to establish they lied, because they responded based on the most common definition?

In terms of "Sexual Relations," it would then be reasonable to use the extreme Islamic sharia law when defining the term – meaning just being in the same room alone with a member of the opposite sex who was not a family member. It could constitute "Sexual Relations."

In your first eight years of life, how were you taught to think? What bias or bigotry was ingrained in your soul?

What childhood constraints control you today?

Grow Up. Or is it that you would prefer not to grow up – that you prefer not to rethink the definitions you were taught as a child? It is, after all, the mindset that caused Bible authors to declare the *"visiting the iniquity of the fathers on the children to the third and the fourth generation of those who hate me."*

In the *Merchant of Venice*, Shakespeare phrased it as "*The sins of the father are to be laid upon the children.*" Those sins being the child of a Jewish father. But then, it was pointed out: "*That were a kind of bastard hope, indeed: so the sins of my mother should be visited upon me.*"

I take it to mean we cannot escape our ancestry. Shakespeare might have been making an "inside joke" based on Ashkenazi practice which holds the Jewishness of a child being inherited from the mother.

The attacks on Trump might be a reversal – where an Orthodox Jewish daughter visits the iniquity upon her father and the attacks on Trump are only antisemitism practiced by jealous Jews who we know as the House Managers led by a Catholic.

There are always ramifications to biased actions. In February, Pelosi had been interviewed about the impeachment and admitted to there being no rush: "*Speed? It's been going on 22 months—two and a half years, actually.*" Though it was interesting that a lack of haste would manifest in her delaying passing the Articles to the Senate at a time when the pandemic was known to be emerging and, if Trump and the media were otherwise occupied, it would force Financial Markets down in the same way the actions against Clinton and Nixon had – a DJIA drop of between 22% to 49%.

Given her behavior opposing impeachment, then supporting it, then holding the Articles until they passed into a new Tax Year, could Pelosi have been seeking to create a "buying opportunity" – first using impeachment and then the backup plan of the pandemic?

The pandemic triggered a DJIA fall from 29,568.57 to 18,213.65 – a loss of 38.4% by the time the stimulus legislation she also delayed was voted on. Did her family do any buying in late March?

CHAPTER FOUR – GEARBOX

"Accumulation of wealth at one pole is at the same time accumulation of misery, agony of toil, slavery, ignorance, brutality, mental degradation, at the opposite pole." ~ Karl Marx

Children often refuse to grow up, they keep with the lessons learned in those first seven years of life and never strive to understand or learn the reason behind the lessons they are taught.

In the Bible, we are told that the sins of the parents are vested on the young for the next three or four generations. It makes sense – because people tend not to question, and they don't question because, in their first seven years, they were taught not to respect their elders and not challenge their wisdom. They are even taught to "do as I say, not as I do."

Comically, the concept behind that "do as I say, not as I do" line is often a parent or elder address the sin and attempting to eradicate it. They cannot change a lifetime habit or perspective that has become second nature, but they also know its wrong and try to change it in the next generation. In other cases, it's pure hypocrisy.

On 23 January, Senator Joni Ernst tweeted: *"The Democratic House Managers' hypocrisy is on full display: they've spent most of their time lecturing the Senate on aid to Ukraine, yet four of them voted AGAINST legislation that provided the very same aid they're lecturing us on."*

During a break in the Manager's reciting receptive hypothetical assertions about random consequences resulting from allowing Trump to remain POTUS until the election, Ernst reminded reporters that Russia had invaded Crimea in 2014, and Obama responded by sending blankets rather than the lethal military aid and assistance provided by Trump, putting it in the current Impeachment context saying: *"What I find very interesting now is that the House Managers are very, very centered on the fact that Russia was invading Ukraine. And military funding to Ukraine."*

We know Biden bragging on C-SPAN: *"..., you've got six hours. If you don't fire that prosecutor, United States will not give you $1 Billion in Aid"* they said he didn't have the authority. As he told it, he implicated Obama in the blackmail by saying, *"if you don't trust me call the president."*

During the House presentation of its case on 22nd and 23rd, Schiff and Nadler each excused the extortion as acceptable because it was "administration policy." Thus, extortion by Trump is alleged to have undertaken is obviously illegal because it is not his official policy toward Ukraine or any other nation. But, violating multiple Federal Laws and endangering the survival of a nation under attack from Russia is perfectly acceptable if it conforms to "administration policy."

In my 2014 book, *'Death over Life, a prophecy of America's destruction'*, where a chapter is devoted to the Crimea and I said: "*The historic sponsor of pogroms is now playing its Jewish card to justify a possible expansion of activities beyond a Crimean boundary and on to the historically disputed Galician territories.*"

As I mention in the chapter preceding the one on the Crimea: "*Following the official lead, journalist Alexander Prokhanov warned: 'I'm especially astonished by the Jewish organizations that support this Maidan. Don't they understand that they are helping bring on a second Holocaust?'*"

Anti-Semitism was seen as an issue, and when we look at the attacks on Trump, it is interesting that the most visible member of his family is his Orthodox Jewish daughter, and Trump is being attacked by Schumer, Schiff and Nadler – all of whom are Jews whose crime is that they are defending Joe Biden's extortion of Ukraine's government by saying it was "administration policy" and was supported "*by others in the Obama administration, as well other Western governments and international lenders.*"

The problem here is that Biden's defenders are invoking what is known as the *"Nuremberg defense"* or "*Superior Orders*" defense that many recognized by the phrase "*I was just following orders*" – it was used to justify the murder of six million Jews and many others, some of whom are now identified as LGBTQ. If the Vice President is actually an insignificant pion whose every act of disobedience could result in his termination, then there is a "*Superior Orders*" argument. But if a Vice President is a high official, then the crime is a high crime.

In the interest of full disclosure, I need to pint out the reality I have discussed in several of my books – I'm Jewish and was raised in a family of Kohanim descended from the tenth century Rashi, Shlomo Yitzchaki, with DNA that is central to the Ashkenazi Levite. So, basically, I'm angered by "family members" using Nazi excuses while they attack someone who was investigating a criminal act by asking the victim for information.   These alleged Democrats, these Jewish Nazis or Russian puppets, are going out of their way to harm America and a Democratic Party I have been a voting member of for 55-years.

The Levite-Kohanim connection, the lessons of my first 7-years, tends to bias me toward Talmudic prophecy and history. With that in mind, as I mention in the 2014 book: *"Historically, Babylon fell to the Persian, Cyrus the Great, then his successor, Darius the Great, was defeated by the Scythians who owned the region of the Crimea and southern Ukraine. That is the historical allusion which is coming into play."*

Today, Persia equates to Iran; the Scythian tactics are inherent in Russian military tactics used against Napoleon and Hitler. But who is the modern Babylon? Is it, as some have asserted, America? In the book I said:

"Toss in the dragon symbol and you can offer up China as the Babylon – but, Beijing isn't part of the 2013-2014 game."

I go on to point out that Russia's best weapon is the American dollar and undermining it through a Russia-China economic alliance which allows the yuan to become the reserve currency – that is, to have China create a New Spice Trade which excludes America. But, as we know with the trade war and subsequent signing of the Phase One agreement, Trump has taken the actions predicted in the early books in this series pointed to the USA and China as joint partners holding control over the mercantile network that will define the 21st-century.

Six years to the day, before the Impeachment hearings, I wrote:

"Putin knows the game, and has indicated his belief that the United States is living way beyond its means and has been hedging its economic problems into the world economy, in the same way that high-risk mortgages were bundled into bonds and contributed to the 2007 economic turmoil – in that analogy, America is parasitically living off the global economy through a dollar-based monopoly."

Trump has been striving to restructure what Reagan's voodoo economics created. However, we have the historic record associated with impeachment based on real statutory crimes – that of Nixon and Clinton.

When Clinton was impeached over "Oral in the Oval", we can look to the DJIA peak at 9,418 on 17 July 1998 and the subsequent fall to 7,360 on 1 September – a loss of 21.8-percent. With Nixon the issue was a DNC headquarters break-in and burglary at the Watergate Office Building in Washington, D.C. on the 17 June 1972; the perpetrators were convicted on 30 January 1973 – in December 1972, the DJIA had peaked 1,020; it then turned downward to 607 in September 1974 – Nixon had resigned the previous month (9 August 1974). This was about a 42-percent loss; in current, inflation-adjusted terms, the loss was closer to 49-percent.

It would take until November 1982, when the nation came out of the Reagan recession, that the DJIA broke the record high made ten years earlier.

We see the House trying to trigger the very economic turmoil that benefits Russia – consistent with Clinton seeking assistance from Russia in 2016, the House is working to achieve the Russian goal that is predicated on crashing the American economy as noted in 2014.

Where is the evidence of extortion?

As annoying as it might seem, the standard we need to use is that set by Biden in his delightful braggadocios timeline inconsistent assertion he told Ukraine officials: "..., *you've got six hours. If you don't fire that prosecutor, United States will not give you $1 Billion in Aid.*"

Biden wasn't in Ukraine in 2016, so how could he personally deliver his extortion ultimatum? Biden lied, but why would he lie about violating multiple Federal Laws and then tack on "*if you don't trust me call the president*"?

Immediately we are told that Obama approved the extortion.

On 24 September 2019, Investigative Reporter John Solomon wrote:

> "*The Obama White House unexpectedly invited Ukraine's top prosecutors to Washington to discuss fighting corruption in the country.*

> "*The meeting, promised as training, turned out to be more of a pretext for the Obama administration to pressure Ukraine's prosecutors to drop an investigation into the Burisma Holdings gas company that employed Hunter Biden and to look for new evidence in a then-dormant criminal case against eventual Trump campaign chairman Paul Manafort, a GOP lobbyist.*"

This also implicates the Obama administration.

Here it's worse, the face-to-face confrontation is removed from Ukraine and placed in Washington D.C. – is it actually in the White House? We aren't told.

However, it is clear that Ukraine is being coerced to stop Shokin from investigating Burisma Holdings. We also learn Valeriy Chaly, the Ambassador of Ukraine to the United States between 2015 and 2019, that in March 2016, a DNC contractor *"pressed his embassy to try to find any Russian dirt on Trump and Manafort that might reside in Ukraine's intelligence files. The DNC contractor also asked Chaly's team to try to persuade Ukraine's president at the time, Petro Poroshenko, to make a statement disparaging Manafort when the Ukrainian leader visited the United States during the 2016 election."*

So we have the Democratic National Committee involved in an attack on Paul Manafort and this would later manifest in the Mueller investigation linking Ukraine to the 2016 election interference.

However, what is being reported about Biden and what House witnesses testified was the Obama Government Policy brings us to the horrifying reality using extortion of foreign governments to influence elections goes back to the 2016 election and does not require Russia to exert interference. And if it did interfere, Russia might well side with the DNC and attempts to crash the economy using impeachment.

We are seeing the gears turn; we are seeing them turn back on themselves. We are also seeing examples of *"Lawyer's Lies"*, evasive distraction, misdirection, obfuscation, or other corrupt legal practices.

Were this simply political, impeachment would be unnecessary. But we know that Rep. Al Green (D-TX) introduced the first motion to impeach resulted in a 364-58 House vote on a *"motion to table"* on 6 December 2017. So two years before Articles of Impeachment passed, the 58 House Democrats were already seeking an excuse to impeach.

Ten-percent of the Texas delegation supported impeachment based on the idea that Trump was *"unfit to be President."* There was no crime, no wrongdoing, no mention of Russia or interference in the 2016 elections, and certainly nothing to do with Biden or Ukraine

Green argued that Trump sowed *"discord among the people of the United States"* and his existence *"harmed the society of the United States."* These are not impeachable assertions, so for two years the House fished around for a justification – it turned out to be one that Biden provided a month after the *"motion to table"* when he brazenly bragged about extortion and coercion of Ukraine to have the foreign official who was investigating Burisma Holdings – supposedly because the Prosecutor General Viktor Shokin was NOT investigating Burisma or corruption.

What we did not hear was that on 18 February 2016, Latvian law enforcement alerted Ukrainian prosecutors – Shokin – they had flagged payments from Burisma Holdings to American accounts that were "*suspicious.*" Those payments included funds paid to the firm owned by Hunter Biden and Devon Archer. This alert was confirmed by Latvian when the matter was pursued by an investigative reporter named John Solomon, who reported the confirmation on 17 December 2019.

In an ABC News interview, Shokin confirmed that just before he was fired as a result of the coercive extortion applied by Joe Biden he also preparing to interview Hunter Biden relative to his connection to the established Burisma corruption – at the time, various Burisma assets were frozen and there was an active investigation.

In 2015, the British government had frozen Burisma assets but in January 2015 the British court was forced to order unfreezing the assets and dismissal of the case because Ukraine's Prosecutor General failed to provide documents needed for the investigation. That was the corrupt individual Viktor Shokin replaced on 10 February 2015.

Vitaly Yarema, the Prosecutor General who failed to provide the required documents, served between 19 June 2014 & 10 February 2015 – the case against Burisma began prior to Yarema's appointment.

Yarema took office after both attorney Hunter Biden and his business partner Devon Archer joined the Burisma board (April 2014).

Archer was the John Kerry's 2004 senior presidential campaign adviser and, at the time Kerry was the United States Secretary of State – a position he held from 1 February 2013 to 20 January 2017. Thus Archer exhibited a close personal connection with the head of the State Department. This is how certain influential gears work and interact.

Shokin could not be bought, so he had to be fired. The State Department attested to the honesty of Burisma, even though its owner Mykola Zlochevsky had been under investigation relative to allegations of money laundering, tax evasion, and corruption during 2010-2012. Concurrent with the hiring of Biden and Archer in April 2014 Ukraine Serious Fraud Office froze approximately $23 million belonging to Zlochevsky or his companies. In January 2015, the charges had to be dropped due to inadequate evidence – it had vanished and a few weeks later Yarema was replaced.

The Burisma matter is complicated and Zlochevsky no longer lives in Ukraine, and his exact whereabouts are unknown. The exact connection between the Biden's and the timeline for Burisma should be investigated – especially given Biden's bragging of the extortion and the obvious timeline overlap or interconnections.

This brings us to Impeachment versus true honest politics and accommodations aimed at achieving the best for the nation.

Fighting Trump is easy, but the House Managers are making it hard. Their problem is they rely upon *"Lawyer's Lies"* – systematic misrepresentation of the truth. In the PIRATES movie, the Johnny Depp character, Captain Sparrow, expresses the idea as *"You lied to me by telling me the truth."*

Growing up in Brooklyn and Queens in the 1950s, there were things that every 'outsider' kid learned – those who were smarter, the kids later called 'geeks', and those who didn't believe in wasting time on trivial nonsense that often defined the schoolyard interactions.

Based on that: Trump's family were successful risk-takers; they dislike war or conflict, so move to win quickly. In previous books in this series, I use the Queens schoolyard rules and those my dad taught me. Donald John Trump plays by those rules; one of which is the idea that confrontation saves time.

Be aggressive, but stay on your side of "the line" – much like the ancient Scythian in their confrontation with *Darius the Great*, where the line was a river, and a Greek Oracle had warned, *"The first one in the River loses."* In the end, the aggressor, the one who attacks first or throws the first punch, always loses.

You can be aggressive, but a variation on *'passive-aggressive'* – Trump uses insulting or belittling nicknames because there is no real mean of countering them. Unless you are a Greta Thunberg and accept the embrace of the attack and go with it, turning it to where you want to go. Become the lead stallion by first running with the herd so they see you as one of them; then run to the front, so they see you as their leader; then be their leader and turn them to where you want them to go.

You've read a lot of this in the earlier books in this series. Thus you know Trump's technique and might have grasped his deep respect for Greta – a girl who has Asperger syndrome, obsessive-compulsive disorder, and a situational speaking disorder called selective mutism – who, at the age of 15, emerged as a Swedish environmental activist demonstrating alone in front of the Swedish Parliament; by the time she was 16, she was the symbol for a global movement and addressing the United Nations, and meeting with heads of state.

Of course, his respect for Greta cannot be overtly expressed – a segment of his political base are *"Climate Deniers"*. Even those seen promoting a Green New Deal (GND) deny many of the realities that are inherent in the current climate change environment – realities like that of Climate Refugees and the need for strong border control that will allow their systematic integration into the social fabric of America.

While the GND fails to address some realities and talks about the climate in terms of gas measurement rather than economics and industrialization for environmental needs. Look at Trump's approach, he seems to stand aside and allow the economy to address climate change while he attacks silly agreements aimed at doing too little too late – just as Greta points out in her speeches.

But the fun is their appreciative exchange as two people who understand the ancient rules. Trump can tweet: *"Greta must work on her anger management problem, then go to a good old fashioned movie with a friend! Chill Greta, Chill!"*

Greta immediately replies that she is: *"A teenager working on her anger management problem. Currently chilling and watching a good old fashioned movie with a friend."*

Greta addressed the realities in terms Donald understands and appreciates when phrased in the impeachment context:

"It's quite hilarious when the only thing people can do is mock you, or talk about your appearance or personality, as it means they have no argument or nothing else to say."

As Greta expresses it, it isn't a Trump characteristic, but rather it is characteristic of a certain mindless demographic for whom focus on appearance – Ivanka's stiletto heels and such – is the only means of attack. For Trump, it's an intentional way to throw an opponent off balance and distract them from the real action; in part, it is related to the idea that you behave in a nonconformist manner, something that doesn't conform to what they are accustomed to.

Again, in earlier books in this series, the opening sequence to **Willy Wonka and the Chocolate Factory** was used in reference to Gene Wilder setting the stage with his initial appearance on screen, which he explains, "*From that time on, no one will know if I'm lying or telling the truth.*" Or maybe, complaints about Trump are better expressed by Charlie Chaplin: "*I remain just one thing, and one thing only, and that is a clown. It places me on a far higher plane than any politician.*"

Following the Queens' schoolyard training of our youth, Trump would have learned you do not start the fight, and you do not lose it. If knocked down, get up; then knock the other guy down, and make damned sure he doesn't get up. If you are going to lose a fight, make sure you win. It sounds contradictory, but lawyers engage in it all the time – they lose a case and their client actually comes out better off than if they had won.

The House Managers stand to gain more if they lose, then if they win and are held responsible for the economic collapse that would follow. When they lose, they are free to yell they were "*cheated*" or the Senate Trial was "*rigged*" against them.

While Schiff and Nadler play childish games and spin Lawyer's Lies to distract their cohort from the fact they lack an honest basis for impeachment, the issues Donald and Greta are addressing continue. In November 2019, climate experts were agreed, the earth was quickly reaching the tipping point stage of the new climate era.

For some, it was "*an existential threat to civilization.*" In terms Trump and China understand: "*No amount of economic cost-benefit analysis is going to help us. We need to change our approach to the climate problem.*"

As times change we lose images that could teach or remind us of how things should work. It comes with a process of dismissing the sins of our parents – a "*baby and bathwater*" thing. But the Donald-Greta exchange is different – recognize why it works. These two are not antagonistic, they are functioning together, though going in what the media reports as opposing directions.

In 1936, Chaplin made a film called "*Modern Times*" in which he gets caught up in a huge gearbox. Think about gears; think about how they work, how they rotate – opposite directions coming together to exchange or transmit energy and motion. But they cannot work if they are rotating in the same direction. Governments work only when the branches come together, even while working different agendas.

Government functions when its branches come together and share or exchange power – when there is a "*Balance of Power*" that is respected. The Trump Impeachment is an example of gross disrespect for the Constitution and *"separation of powers."*

Trump is a gear. His whole life has been defined by elements of conflict at the point of contact. And assuming the other gear wants to function optimally – negotiating the exchange of power as promised by *USMCA* and the *Phase-One* China Trade agreement.

Those who oppose, like the impeachment crackpots who started their nonsense on 9 November 2016, and House Managers who lie and misrepresent reality, will if they succeed in an attempt to rotate down while Trump goes up, stop the machinery.

A conviction would catch the financial markets by surprise and trigger a financial crash of gargantuan proportions – leading to a truly Great Depression. It would be much wiser to behave like Greta, and turn the Trump energy to their own use; gain strength by going with it and thereby becoming accomplish the stuff of legend.

Greta Thunberg is a modern Joan D'Arc whose Hundred Year War is defined by Climate Change and not military conflict. Both of these young ladies entered history around the age of 15 and began to be a clear influence by the time they were 17. At the age of 19, Joan of Arc, "The Maid of Orléans", was executed by the English; it is unlikely such a fate would befall Greta, even though she is confronting world leaders and demanding they do something meaningful in terms of the climate gas effects her cousin codified in his formula.

As was being reported in late 2019 and early 2020, the Paris Climate Accord signatories were actually making things worse – they shifted their pollution to underdeveloped nations located in the worst possible places on the planet for introducing additional climate gases and it was showing in both the metrics and weather reports.

Trump took another route. He renegotiated trade agreements in a way that would encourage Green Energy firms to relocate or to be created in the United States. He cheered coal, but that was a tactic to assure those still working in that shrinking industry of job security, even as the coal companies changed over to renewable energy areas.

The GND is a Bernie Sanders thing, and in other areas, Trump had no problem referring to him as "crazy Bernie" whenever an idea lacked the necessary economic foundation. But, in February 2020, when Hillary Clinton attacked Sanders, Trump spoke of him in a way similar to that used with Greta: *"I like Bernie, I wish Bernie well. It will be interesting to see how he does. I think what happened to*

Bernie maybe was not so nice. I think he was taken advantage of. He ran great four years ago, and he was not treated with respect by Clinton."

Bernie is not a Potus Cousin, he's not a descendant of the five-sisters, and allowing for his age and heart attack, he wouldn't be a viable nominee – though being a nominee would enhance his standing in the Senate and, if he's smart, Sanders could push a positive climate and social agenda that Trump would love to make a part of his legacy.

There are basics that must be done to address climate issues. If Congress wanted to act, instead of blaming others for their inaction, it would be simple and political. They would place a price on carbon or other climate emissions products; end depletion allowances that are basically needless tax shelters; stop the construction of coal-powered plants; tax carbon or other climate gases and facilitate the installation of point of use solar or wind electric generation and storage.

Impeachment requires a Standardization of an action. Actions must be defined by Objective Standards universally applied. Abuse of Power has no definition or standardized criteria. Per Allan Dershowitz said, on 27 January, that a charge based on the "Abuse of Power" is itself unconstitutional because it fails to meet the primary test of one that is sufficiently standardized to be objectively determined.

"Trust, Truth, Honesty, and Right" are moral, not legal, terms. A fair and unbiased prosecution would require an objective criterion – one that does NOT result in any President being subject to removal at the whim off a Congressional majority.

Allan Dershowitz proposed a "Shoe Test" – put the shoe on the other foot and apply the same facts to a member of the opposite party and ask if the determination would remain the same.

In a very real way, Allan Dershowitz was imposing the Golden Rule: *"Do not do unto your neighbor what you would not have done to you."*

The gears were turning and the goal of Adam Schiff was to lock them. To have witnesses to do what the House failed to do yet claimed it had done. As gears turn, on 30 January, a Senate Q&A wrapped up and *"The Biden Rule"*, named after a Joe Biden speech in connection with the Merrick Garland Supreme Court nomination: *"a process that is already in doubt in the minds of many will become distrusted by all."* In an election year, let the people vote first.

CHAPTER FIVE – THE BIG LIE

"Republicans know that the facts are damning for Donald Trump. If they push through a sham trial to protect him, with no witnesses and no White House documents, they will be assisting with his cover-up, and setting a terrible precedent for the future of our country."
~ Elizabeth Warren 31 January 2020

Strange how the gears turn.

The 2019 impeachment originated with Joe Biden's bragging comes around to his once asserting, in an election year, decisions by the Senate should be delayed to allow the people to vote first.

Granted, it was the *Biden Rule* associated with a 2016 Supreme Court nomination, but it is still interesting that it should be brought upon the conclusion of the Senate Q&A.

In the same Q&A Warren posed a question read into the record by Supreme Court Justice John Roberts: *"The question from Sen. Warren is for the House managers: 'At a time when large majorities of Americans have lost faith in government, does the fact that the chief justice is presiding over an impeachment trial in which Republican senators have thus far refused to allow witnesses or evidence contribute to the loss of legitimacy of the chief justice, the Supreme Court, and the Constitution?'"*

Is any witness going to support House Manager Adam Schiff claiming that the telephone conversation consisted of Trump telling Zelensky: *"I will give you military dollars if you will give me help in my reelection, if you will give me illicit foreign interference in our election"*?

Schiff lied. He knew he was engaged in telling lies and persisted in accordance with the Goebbels principle: *"Repeat a lie often enough and it becomes the truth."* Schiff begins every speech with the lie, then speaks as if he is providing evidence when he is really obfuscating.

Joe Biden can brag about telling Ukraine officials, *"I'm leaving in six hours, you've got six hours. If you don't fire that prosecutor, United States will not give you $1 Billion in Aid..."* and that's legal; It's perfectly acceptable because, as Biden said, *"if you don't trust me call the president."*

President Obama was interviewed after the Shokin firing.

Obama was asked about aid to Ukraine and said "it's possible" – that upset Ukraine officials who then felt they had fired Shokin for nothing.   What the Obama interview revealed was that the loan guarantee had not been appropriated when Biden used it in his extortion scheme. There was nothing to cancel, for the simple reason nothing had been approved by Congress.

So the President – the position now held by Donald J Trump – can authorize extortion on a six-hour clock or completely cancel an appropriation. But only if it is a Democratic POTUS can they do that.

Schiff's logic and the impression he promoted was that Barack Obama had the authority to override the Impoundment Control Act of 1974 and completely cancel funds. But if the funds guarantee had not yet been authorized, then the law was not in play. We also know that when Schiff repeated the witness statements about "Administrative Policy," he was promoting *"lawyers lie"* – inferring that extortion was Obama policy.

As stated by Obama in a videotaped 9 February 2015 interview: *"We occasionally have to twist the arms of countries that wouldn't do what we need them to do if it weren't for the various economic or diplomatic or in some cases military leverage that we have."*

So, as we could logically expect, there are contexts where we can hold extortion to be an accepted political policy – but in all cases, there would some political benefit served which introduces a *"lawyers lie."* As we know, that means a truth that can be taken two ways – one of which allows it to be a lie. If Trump used the investigation for political benefit, it was and is accepted American policy – only with Trump, there is no evidence, certainly no brazen admission, of the monetary extortion and related guilt seen with Biden using it to fire a Prosecutor investigating his son's employer and about to open an investigation on his son, Hunter.

Obama's stated policy does not allow the extortion. Did Obama even know about it in terms of the Burisma investigation? What were they speaking of as "Administrative Policy" or "Government Policy"? Biden was point-man coordinating American assistance in Ukraine's fight against systemic corruption – but as the UkraineGate evidence shows, Biden was an integral part of it; his son, one former Ukraine official stated, was the conduit for bribes to Joe Biden.

Is it true? How would we know without a detailed and honest investigation?

Clearly, the facts will remain concealed and the Truth will never be learned – so long as anti-Trump propaganda protects Biden.

So Obama was not part of the extortion, and the Government Policy was an aid in ending corruption, which Biden had used to profit from that corruption and obtain a million a year income for Hunter to do nothing except allow his an opportunity to abuse his authority and promote the corruption the President wanted to end.

No authority can be delegated to the Vice President and used at his desecration to commit extortion. However, Adam Schiff actually promoted the idea that it could be combined with lies then used to fire the Prosecutor investigating and freezing assets of the firm where the Vice President's son is a member of the Board of Directors.

When dealing this in the context of Presidential Impeachment over a President asking the victim for any evidence in the investigation they are conducting which mention either the Biden name or that of the CrowdStrike investigation into the 2016 hacking of DNC servers, we are dealing with wanting to impeach a POTUS for enforcing the law.

It's interesting that neither Prosecutor Adam Schiff nor Law Professor Elizabeth Warren could take the time to reference *18 U.S. Code § 208. Acts affecting a personal financial interest.* And that neither paid any attention to what was happening in Ukraine.

Had they done so, they would have discovered, with a focus on applicable data:

(a) Except as permitted by subsection (b) hereof, whoever, being an officer...of the executive branch of the [U. S.] Government,... participates personally...,or organization with whom he is negotiating [where they or family member] has any arrangement concerning prospective employment, has a financial interest..."

As was pointed out, there are numerous sections that may apply or which a competent lawyer could argue does not apply to foreign extortion of the type involving Ukraine, Shokin, and Hunter Biden. But Schiff and all but three House Democrats have already had a vote in which they asserted a *quid pro quo* extortion, using federal funds, is a disqualification for the Oval Office – unless you are Joe Biden.

It's important to note that when Biden made his brag he was not a candidate; when Rudy Giuliani went to Ukraine to investigate the background information supporting the Brag, Biden was still not a candidate. More important, we have the fact that the mater was handled quietly and the facts were being gathered in the appropriate manner; it was the mysterious uninvolved whistleblower, Adam Schiff, and Jerry Nadler who made things public and brought them front and center in the media. Ukraine was conducting its investigations, the former Prosecutor General had brought two cases related to the firing and during the Senate Impeachment Trial filed a complaint under Ukraine law which, if acted upon, opens investigations into everything the Biden name was associated with.

Every corrupt firm and individual Hunter or Joe spoke to would now be a target for Ukraine's anti-corruption forces. Anyone who was a partner or associate of Hunter will be investigated and the *"follow the money"* concept will define some aspects of the investigations.

If we look to the Senate Record, Patrick F. Philbin presented the timeline facts during the Q&A:

"...there is other information publicly available and in the record that I think is important for understanding the timeline and understanding why it was that the information related to the Bidens and the Burisma affair came up when it did.

"...President Poroshenko was the person who Joe Biden himself went to to have the prosecutor fired. So as long as President Poroshenko was still in charge in Ukraine, he was the person who Joe Biden had spoken to to get the prosecutor, Shokin, fired when, according to public reports, Shokin was looking into Burisma. As long as he was still the President in Ukraine, it questioned the utility of raising an incident in which he was the one who was taking the direction from Vice President Biden to fire the prosecutor.

"... we have heard a lot about Rudy Giuliani, the President's private lawyer, and what was he interested in Ukraine and what was his role? ...had been asking a lot of questions in Ukraine dating back to the fall of 2018, and in November 2018, he said publicly he was given some tips about things to look into.

"He gave a dossier to the State Department in March of [2019].

"Remember, Vice President Biden announced his candidacy in April – April 25. In March, Rudy Giuliani gave documents to the State Department, including interview notes from interviews he conducted both with Shokin and with Yuriy Lutsenko, who was also a prosecutor in Ukraine. Those interview notes are from January 23 and January 25, 2019 – so months before Vice

President Biden announced any candidacy – and it goes through in these interview notes, Shokin explaining that he was removed at the request of Mr. Joseph Biden, the Vice President.

"Months before Vice President Biden announced his candidacy, Mr. Giuliani is looking into this issue, interviewing people, and getting information about it.

"In addition, in March of 2019, articles began to be published. Then three articles were published by ABC, by the New Yorker, and by the Washington Post before the July 25 call.

"On July 22, 3 days before the call, the Washington Post has an article specifically about the Bidens and Burisma. That is what makes it suddenly current, relevant, probably to be in someone's mind."

Accepting the existence of a record of the dossier being at the State Department the month before Biden announced his candidacy, there is clear evidence that there was no political rival context at all.

Then, there is the logical problem of the House assertion that Biden is or was a rival when he announced and when the telephone call happened. Biden is a candidate and his real rivals were twenty-four other Democrats who had also announced. As the final stage of the Senate Trial was occurring, when a motion for additional witnesses and documents was defeated 51:49 Biden still had to pass muster in the Iowa caucus – the first in the nomination process. Until 13 July 2020 when the Democrats hold their Nominating Convention, Biden is not and cannot be the Democratic rival to Republican Trump.

If we look at the Schiff statements in the same Senate record, we see him misrepresent the facts in the same way he has throughout the impeachment process: *"I would suggest to you that for a President to turn to his Justice Department and say, 'I want you to investigate my political rival,' taints whatever investigation they do. Presidents should not be in the business of asking even their own Justice Department to investigate their rivals."*

At no time did, or could, the President have asked the Justice Department *"to investigate my political rival"*. The facts show that it was Giuliani who [quietly} gathered the relevant data long before Biden announced himself to be a candidate; Giuliani then turned the documents over to the State Department a month BEFORE Biden announced.

Throughout the process and Transcript rendition, Schiff lied.

Adam Schiff intentionally lied to Congress – House and Senate – and the American public. Granted, except when giving renditions of transcripts – which were blatant falsehoods – he generally relied upon *"Lawyer's Lies,"* obfuscation, distraction, or irrelevant hypothetical.

As was evident, even to media pundits favoring impeachment, on 30 January Schiff was actively delaying the obvious Trial resolution so that Senatorial rivals to Biden were prevented from campaigning in Iowa during the last two days available before the caucus vote.

Schiff's actions hampered Biden's true campaign rivals. Pete Buttigieg was not hampered and took the lead over Bernie Sanders – even while Sanders received the most votes and had effectively repeated the Trump-Clinton relationship. But even with the obvious campaign access advantage, Biden was forced to admit he was *"Gut Punched"* when all he achieved was a dismal fourth place.

Counsel Jay Sekulow responded to several questions including the one concerning Schiff's "political rival" assertion. Note that he does not debate the "rival" issue, even though the facts in the record said that the relationship did not exist:

"He said it would be targeting a rival. That is what that did. He said it would be calling for foreign assistance in that. In the particular facts of Crossfire Hurricane, it has been well established now that, in fact, Fusion GPS utilized the services of a former foreign intelligence officer, Christopher Steele, to put together a dossier and that Christopher Steele relied on his network of resources around the globe, including Russia and other places, to put together this dossier, which then James Comey said was unverified and salacious. Yet it was the basis upon which the Department of Justice and the FBI obtained FISA warrants. This was in 2016, against a rival campaign. So we don't have to do hypotheticals. It is precisely the situation."

Why concede that Biden was the political rival before he even announced that he was running for President?

Why fight a semantic battle?

Biden is a Democrat and Trump a Republican – the two parties are rivals. The Democrats appeared to have been rigging the debate process so that women and minorities would be limited or excluded – an allegation leveled by Tulsi Gabbard, who falls into both categories. The Republicans know this to be true and that the Senate Trial – that Pelosi delaying the transmission of Articles of Impeachment to the

Senate – was timed to create a campaign conflict for Biden's Senate rivals. Having delayed sending the Impeachment documents to the Senate, Pelosi was attacked by a fellow Democrat who was also Senator from her own state, Senator Dianne Feinstein (D-Calif.): *"The longer it goes on the less urgent it becomes. So if it's serious and urgent, send them over. If it isn't, don't send it over."*

This attack was foundational. The process had been rushed and was incomplete because, supposedly, as Rep. John Lewis (D-Ga) said when the hearings were announced: *"To delay or to do otherwise would betray the foundation of our democracy."*

With the goal to *"betray the foundation of our democracy,"* it follows that Pelosi would delay the Articles of Impeachment for almost a month so the propaganda system could assert a case the House could not make.

Remember during the investigative impeachment process in the House, the point repeatedly made was that the matter was so serious as to require it be expedited and therefore they could not wait for the proper legal process to play out. But then, when the Impeachment vote succeeded, Nancy Pelosi saw no contradiction delaying the final Articles of Impeachment being transferred to the Senate – effectively committing ARTICLE II: OBSTRUCTION OF CONGRESS.

Once the matter had reached the Senate, the New York Times released information purported to be in a yet to be released biography, *'The Room Where It Happened: A White House Memoir'*, by John Bolton, who allegedly claimed Trump had explicitly stated he was going to demand a qui pro quo between Ukraine aid and investigating Biden.

While not scheduled for release until 17 March 2020, the book's pre-publication sales propelled it to #1 Best Seller status on Amazon. In theory, the manuscript was to undergo a security clearance, so who released the pages to the New York Times?

Both Bolton and his publisher, Simon & Schuster, were quick to deny any responsibility; speaking through their attorney, Charles Cooper they said: *"It is clear, regrettably, from The New York Times article published today that the prepublication review process has been corrupted and that information has been disclosed by persons other than those involved in reviewing the manuscript."*

At a minimum, the "leak" meant sales of about 1,100 copies per day for both the eBook and Print editions; the eBook listed at $16.99, while the Hardcover was originally priced at \$32.50, but by the end of the first week, it was discounted to \$19.50. With the certainty there would be no testimony, plus publicity generated by the Senate debates, the sales continued to grow.

Prior to the Times story, Bolton had been careful to assert he would be willing to testify before the Senate. Impeachment pundits used that as a nod to credibility – *"willingness to state under oath."*

But, the Senate voted not to conduct the House investigation for them and declined to call witnesses; Adam Schiff then revealed: *"We did approach John Bolton's counsel, asked if Mr. Bolton would be willing to submit an affidavit under oath, describing what he observed in terms of the President's Ukraine misconduct, and he refused. For whatever reason, he apparently was willing to testify before the Senate, but apart from that, seems intent on saving it for his book."*

Because the book was not scheduled for release until March, it also became a useful tool for speculation and hypothetical projection of the type typical of corrupt prosecutors whose cases lack any credible evidence. These are the types of attorney who practice *"Lawyer's Lies"* and conform to those described by Johnny Depp in PIRATES: *"You lied to me by telling me the truth."* They are individuals who present the truth in a way that supports their case when, in proper context, it refutes it. As Bolton knew, you can volunteer and gain those optics when you know you will never be called to perform.

Curiously and rather hypocritically, in Iowa Joe Biden declare *"We chose Truth over Lies!"* But the nation has been submitted to months of Schiff delivering lie after lie to brush off Biden's bragging about his Ukraine extortion while asserting Trump was investigating that brag for political gain, even though the entered FACTS show the investigation began well before Biden said he was entering the race.

I'm reminded of the great line delivered by Jack Nicholson in the 1992 film, *"A Few Good Men"*, where, in response to being told *"I want the truth,"* his character, Col. Nathan Jessup, responds sharply with: *"You can't handle the truth!"*

In allowing the persistent lies and misrepresentations by Schiff and Nadler, America's Democrats and California-New York City media have persistently shown they do not want the truth.

In the film, the Jessup character is talking about reality and speaking of the death that brought about the investigation, says: *"That*

Santiago's death, while tragic, probably saved lives." As we know, on 3 January 2020, a United States drone killed Iranian major general Qasem Soleimani of the Islamic Revolutionary Guard Corps – the man behind many terrorist activities who coordinated operations with terrorists, including the one who died with him. Santiago-Soleimani interchangeable fiction and reality where Trump might be Jessup.

Jessup goes on to say: "*You don't want the truth. Because deep down, in places you don't talk about at parties, you want me on that wall. You need me there.*"

Well, Trump does have the Wall that was, since 2006, the Bush-Obama Fence. The purpose of the Wall – not the Fence that Reagan denounced in 1980 and which the Democrats had wanted since before that time – the Wall is aimed at addressing a major Climate Change issue that scientists tell us will be most evident after 2025. True, we know Trump has some aspects of it a "hoax", but he also suggested Solar Collectors be mounted on the Wall to provide clean energy.

It's Trump's style to address a reality – such as Climate Change – that is not openly accepted by one demographic. Trump recognizes both the reality and economic prosperity associated with renewable energy. He wants energy independence that comes with his suggesting renewable energy. Those of us who understand the security reality, in terms of a military threat, also want the renewable energy to be a point of use generation with excess energy fed into the broader grid.

There is that truth. Fighting Trump is easy, he's easy to control – all you need to do is actually listen to what he says, rather than what you want him to have said so you can attack him for it. The impeachment is attacking Trump for "*A Perfect Call.*"

As I am endeavoring to show, if you actually pay attention to the timeline and what was said, Trump was NOT, as Schiff would have you believe, investigating a political rival. Trump was investigating a former Elected Official who bragged about committing extortion of Ukrainian officials. The motive doesn't matter – the media had picked up on it and made it sound "*horrible.*"

What did Trump do? Did he do a Tweet rampage attacking Biden based on media reports, or did he quietly have Rudy Giuliani go and investigate? Then, when there was background data filed with the State Department, and the media was still issuing stories, we had the congratulatory phone call in which the issue was raised.

During the Q&A on 30 January, Senator Susan Collins of Maine asked both parties: *"Are there legitimate circumstances under which a President could request a foreign country to investigate a U.S. citizen, including a political rival, who is not under investigation by the U.S. government? If so, what are they and how do they apply to the present case?"*

The day before Delaware Senator Jeffries had denounced the idea that *"President Trump pressured a foreign government to target an American citizen..."* for investigation. Then, a bit later House Manager Nadler again attacked Trump for *"using his official favor to corruptly benefit himself rather than the American people."* That *"favor"* was a less than formal request that Ukraine to share anything its corruption investigation turns up that has the Biden or Crowdstrike names linked to it with the Attorney General.

Nadler also asserted Trump had *"illegally withholding military aid"* – but, while there is a 1974 law that makes such action illegal, the House Articles of Impeachment do not include the criminal charge.

Nadler was either pointing to the gross incompetence of those who drafted the Articles or the Articles reflect the fact that the law had not been violated – therefore Nadler was again lying to the Senate.

As we know, an actual crime cited in the Articles would have nullified many of the Constitutional arguments put forward by Alan Dershowitz. Yet there were no crimes cited and the House Managers argued they need no have a crime in order to impeach – but, as with Johnson, Nixon, and Clinton, it certainly would have made life easier. If there were clear criminal acts, as there were with Nixon, they might even have gotten Trump to resign – but no crimes were committed, no crimes were charged, so Schiff and Nadler just lied to the Senate and American public. Then the media lapped up those lies and regurgitate them to the public with *"sprinkles on top."*

On 28 January, Attorney and former Ukraine Prosecutor Viktor Shokin filed a formal complaint against Joseph R Biden for violation of *"article 214 of the Criminal Procedure Code of the Ukraine"* which alleged:

During the period 2014-2016, the Prosecutor General's Office of Ukraine was conducting a preliminary investigation into a series of serious crimes committed by the former Minister of Ecology of Ukraine Mykola Zlotchevsky and by the managers of the company "Burisma Holding Limited "(Cyprus), the board of directors of which included, among others, Hunter Biden, son of Joseph Biden, then vice-president of the United States of America.

The investigation into the above-mentioned crimes was carried out in strict accordance with Criminal Law and was under my personal control as the Prosecutor General of Ukraine.

Owing to my firm position on the above-mentioned cases regarding their prompt and objective investigation, which should have resulted in the arrest and the indictment of the guilty parties, Joseph Biden developed a firmly hostile attitude towards me which led him to express in private conversations with senior Ukrainian officials, as well as in his public speeches, a categorical request for my immediate dismissal from the post of Attorney General of Ukraine in exchange for the sum of US $ 1 billion in as a financial guarantee from the United States for the benefit of Ukraine.

The facts I have described above are confirmed, among other things, by the official interview of Joseph Biden published in the media, where he declares that Ukraine will not receive money if I remain in my post as Attorney General.

For all the extortion assertions made against Trump by Schiff, there were NO CRIMINAL CHARGES filed by the House in support of their Articles of Impeachment. However, Biden's action violated Ukraine law and, as we saw in Book 7 of this series, Biden's bragging was effectively a confession to violation of multiple Federal Laws.

Schiff and Nadler have defended Biden's actions as Government Policy. And they claimed it was to attack a political rival. However, it had been established: *"Mayor Giuliani began investigating Ukraine corruption and interference in the 2020 election way back in November of 2018 – a full 6 months before Vice President Biden announced his candidacy and 4 months before the release of the Mueller report,..."* {Senate Record Vol. 166, No. 17} This, therefore, eliminates the political connection argument and again indicates the nature of Schiff and Nadler misrepresentation of facts.

In what they call *"UkraineGate"*, French media has attacked the "fallacy of the narrative launched by Biden's communication advisors" which asserted Shokin's investigation was dormant. They point to a 7 July 2016 post on the official Prosecutor General website which says there was a *"large-scale criminal tax evasion scheme, to which ex-*

Minister M Zlochevsky is involved." And the investigation timeframe was exactly that which Biden propagandists asserted investigations were "stalled" by Shokin.

On 10 October 2016, Shokin's successor affirmed a *"tax audit concerned the period of 8 months of 2016and establishes a violation of tax law."* These audits of Burisma were what Biden had attempted to disrupt. The story goes on to assert American ambassador Pyatt had lied about Shokin *"thwarting a British money-laundering probe into Burisma's owner"* – however that was in 2014, and before Shokin took office, and therefore the US Ambassador to Ukraine Geoffrey Pyatt had apparently willfully lied to defame Shokin to protect Biden.

However, the Pyatt statement was actually misrepresented by American media. Pyatt addressed the enormity of the task Shokin had been given in his directly overseeing of 11,293 investigators, 80% of whom were actors involved in actual corruption. In the French report, Pyatt is shown on video expressing the honest story, stating:

"The United States wants to work with Prosecutor General Shokin so the PGO is leading the fight against corruption."

As shown, the facts contradict the lies Schiff and Nadler have propagated against Shokin in their effort to defend Biden against those words he free declared which constitute a full confession of *quid pro quo* criminal extortion. Moreover, the French story shows that over 31 days the Washington Post used the same false copy-paste narrative in 52 articles by multiple writers beginning around 23 September so as to be timed to the impeachment hearings. Full 38% of those pro-Biden articles which served to attack Trump were produced in the first four days between 23 and 27 September, spread across by-lines of 15 journalists.

The French report traces the anti-Shokin copy-past narrative to a 7 May 2019 Bloomberg declaration that *"Timeline in Ukraine Probe Casts Doubt on Giuliani's Biden Claim."*

We then learn that Vitaliy Kasko, mentioned in Chapter 2, had aligned himself with the Bidens in exchange for the promise he would be the new Prosecutor General. This infers the Joe Biden was actually manipulating the Prosecutor General Office (PGO) the internal affairs. Then we learn that *"around June or July of 2015"* Pyatt told Shokin Burisma *"has to be "handled with 'White Gloves', which implied do nothing."* ABC TV had the facts from Shokin and suppressed them.

A videotaped interview has Shokin producing documentation of 6 ongoing investigations Biden wanted stopped, and on 1 November 2016, Shokin's successor Lutsenko *"stopped all the criminal cases"* because they were all reaching the point where Hunter Biden would be investigated. The ABC reporter who buried the facts would be the one to later interview President Zelensky, and the French show the tape of him trying to force the Ukraine President to call Trump corrupt so it would be on video to use to attack Trump and defend Biden.

The French then show a female CNN reporter manipulating the President's words to infer that *"no one CAN put pressure on me"* was really saying Trump pressured me because it wasn't stated as *"no one DID put pressure on me."*

The French report then confirms part of Biden's brag using a 5 October 2019 Los Angeles Times article that said:

"In the eight days before Shokin was fired in March 2016, Biden phoned Poroshenko four times to reiterate the U.S. position, former aides said. The Ukraine leaders finally relented, and Shokin was sacked."

As the documentary states, Biden obtained what he wanted and he delivered the $1 Billion, *"albeit not in 6 hours but in 5 months."* As we know from the report, it was also done by phone and not face-to-face as falsely presented in the C-SPAN confession which was phrased to allow Biden to claim it was just a story, because his travel log would prove he wasn't in Ukraine in 2016.

But we also learned the New York Times reported the firing of Shokin pleased oligarch Zlochevsky – the new prosecutor, following orders Biden gave Ukraine President Poroshenko, closed the cases. It follows that Zlochevsky would be happy – he had fled the country to escape prosecution and could now return. Shokin then filed a case in Ukrainian Courts, later brought to the European Court of Human Rights, and now has filed the criminal charges against Biden.

We are told in the French report Biden should be investigated because, *"since the investigations were moving forward, he defacto helped the oligarch,..."* and now there will be an investigation of sorts. George Kent, Senior Anti-Corruption Coordinator (2014/15), Deputy of Mission in Ukraine (2015/18) – on 15 October 2019 – gave closed-door testimony to Congress where he revealed he raised the conflict of interest associated with the Bidens and Burisma in February 2015.

Kent addressed talking points of the IMF and European Union siding with the removal of Shokin, stating the United States was the dominant voice they mimicked. As we know, 18 witnesses appeared in the House Impeachment with only Kent's testimony concealed – the transcript obtained for the investigative report shows Kent would have blown a hole in every argument Schiff raised to cover for Biden.

This brings us back to the Q&A by Senator Susan Collins and then to the response by Adam Schiff: "*It may be appropriate for the Justice Department, acting independently and in good faith, to initiate an investigation. There is a process for doing that. We heard testimony about doing that. You can make a request under the mutual legal assistance treaty, MLAT, process when a foreign country has evidence involving a criminal case involving a U.S. person. There is a legitimate way to do that.*"

Under MLAT, everything goes through the Attorney General.

Trump made the connection twice: 1 . "*whatever you can do with the Attorney General would be great*"; 2. "*I would like to have the Attorney General call you or your people and I would like you to get to the bottom of it.*"

MLAT, (22 July 1998) "*Article 2 provides for the establishment of Central Authorities and defines Central Authorities for purposes of the Treaty. For the United States, the Central Authority shall be the Attorney General or a person designated by the Attorney General. For Ukraine, the Central Authority shall be the Ministry of Justice and the Office of the Prosecutor General.*"

Schiff persists in his "Lawyers Lies", but was trapped when he was confronted by Senator Susan Collins' question; his answer served to underscore his primary lie throughout the Impeachment. Trump's call was perfect and invoked MLAT Arrival 2 – but in a way that kept the Biden matter "private" until Schiff politicized it.

There were two possible interpretations of Biden's brag: 1. the "leverage" Obama mentioned which Trump could also legally engage in; 2. Biden seeking personal benefit through his son's million dollar a year income for nothing beyond providing access to his father.

Schiff allegedly coached the Whistleblower so the call would go public – then he knowing and illegally disclosed classified data. But, by phrasing the request to flag data as a favor, Trump was endeavoring to keep the data confidential until such time as it was learned of option

1 or 2 applied. Only Option 2 is illegal – that illegality is the basis for the Ukraine criminal action sought by prosecutor Shokin.

Schiff acted as a dishonest prosecutor when he flat-out lied and misrepresented the call contents – he knew about MLAT, so he knew he was lying. Part of the *"Lawyer Lies"* technique is semantics – with Clinton it was the definition of *"Sexual Relations"*, normally phrased as intercourse and not genital touching, invoked MLAT on an informal level, we have the reality of Trump doing things correctly.

And that leads us to Professor Alan Dershowitz's point: *"When you look at the fullness of the record of their witnesses – their witnesses – the witnesses' statements, the transcripts – there is one thing that emerged: There is no violation of law. There is no violation of the Constitution. There is a disagreement on policy decisions."*

Or, as routinely emerged in the House arguments, "semantics."

Weeks before Dershowitz expressed the legal reality, Speaker Pelosi contradicted the factual reality of their actions: *"The American people deserve the truth. Every Senator now faces a choice: to be loyal to the President or the Constitution. The GOP Senate must immediately proceed in a manner worthy of the Constitution and in light of the gravity of the President's unprecedented abuses. No one is above the law, not even the President."* - 3 January press Release

Remember Col. Jessup? *"You can't handle the truth!"* And the truth is there was nothing there except lies and irrational hypothetical assertions designed to help Schiff distract from a lack of evidence.

On 24 September she had asserted *"The president has admitted to asking the president of Ukraine to take actions which would benefit him politically."* As we now know from the mounting evidence of Biden's interference with Ukraine's legal system.

Yet, when we see the excuses leveled to protect Biden, the idea that "Government Policy" negates the Federal Law, it becomes rather interesting that Pelosi introduced her catchphrase slogan: *"No one is above the law."*

What would Pelosi assert when Shokin's criminal filing results in the investigation whose findings Trump referenced. The House and anti-Trump media have consistently taken the position that Joe Biden was above the law – that he was free to brag about using extortion to have Shokin fired and was free to lie about Shokin shelving Burisma or other corruption investigations.

On the other hand, If Biden and this 'defense' witnesses were correct about Shokin, his National Bureau of Investigation filing will be dismissed as having no merit; if Shokin was actually investigating Burisma, it gives Ukraine a legal basis for investigating both Hunter and Joe Biden, along with Burisma.

Readers should recall that the 25 July Ukraine phone call was 'classified' when Schiff lied or misrepresented its contents to his fellow Congressmen. It was Adam Schiff, not Donald Trump, who used the phone call and Biden's boastful confession of criminality for political purposes in violation of *18 U.S. Code § 798 - Disclosure of classified information* which states: *"(a) Whoever knowingly and willfully communicates, …, or otherwise makes available to an unauthorized person, or publishes, or uses in any manner prejudicial to the safety or interest of the United States…"* That it might have been mistakenly classified does not negate the willful disregard for the law as shown by Schiff throughout his general approach to matters that can be seen as *"prejudicial to the safety or interest of the United States."*

We also know the anti-American cabal used the call expressly for the purpose of initiating the impeachment; California, Texas, and New York City House members began to promote impeachment when the election results were announced on 9 November 2016.

Curiously, the only thing which could really be accomplished would be elevating Mike Pence to the status of POTUS. As shown in the Nixon and Clinton impeachments, financial markets approach impeachment or any loss of a national leader as a negative.

JFK was elected 9 November 1960, when the markets had fallen about 15-percent over the prior ten-months and bottomed just before the election. His first year was marked by a 25-percent climb and then in December 1961 the gains were given back as America became active in Vietnam; in late-summer of 1962, Russia started to have problems.

The cracks in the Communist system trigger a run-up of nearly 70-percent between June 1962 and January 1966. The assassination of JFK occurred on 22 November 1963 without causing a noticeable blip. Even a violent death in office can be taken in stride – if the Vice President is a 4-dot descendant of the four-sisters.

We can assume so as to have a weak opponent in 2020 – in so doing, they also showed their blatant disregard for the economic and political survival of America. Making their effort position precisely consistent with the goals of the nation's enemies.

CHAPTER SIX – INVESTIGATE

"Math is not about memorizing formulas without meaning, but rather about learning how to reason logically through precise statements." ~ Dr. Po-Shen Loh, Carnegie Mellon University

In the quote, Dr. Loh was speaking of quadratic equations and how they frustrate many students. But he was talking about it in the context of confirming that the ancient Babylonians had solved the important equation form, and utilized them, thousands of years ago.

Ancient knowledge was, in many ways, as advanced as modern knowledge – and you understand that when you stay in context. For the Babylonians and Greeks studied by Dr. Loh, their understanding was limited because their math was limited to positive numbers. We use concepts that include zero, negative numbers, and esoteric ideas about imaginary numbers — the square roots of negative numbers.

When we look at politics, the ancient Greeks had democracies, with mandatory participation, in the fifth-century BCE. An Athenian leader, Cleisthenes, introduced demokratia ("rule by the people") in 507 B.C.E. – at a time when the Persian Empire was at its peak and in control of the same Muslim regions now subject to immigration bans; the remains of that Empire are now called Iran and included what is now known as Crimea.

While the scope of quadratic equations has changed and we are experiencing the interaction between Democracy and Empire in the defining of global relations. Yet have we still haven't learned *"how to reason logically through precise statements."* We buy into *"Lawyer's Lies"* and willingly praise *"The Emperor's New Clothes,"* they tell us what we should see, and if we see it we are deemed wise, if we report what is actually there, we deemed fools. We are also told to ignore the ramifications of seeing those magical clothes – ridding ourselves of the President so that the Vice President can be elevated. It is important to note that they do not want to rid us of the administration, they want a religious conservative with no economic background or credentials.

CNN praised Clinton for apologizing for committing perjury after he committed adultery. They condemned Trump for his failure to apologize for not committing any defined crimes – his malfeasance? Trump had the audacity to seek data on a former High Federal Official who bragged about committing extortion which qualified as multiple felonies if they were found to have benefitted a family member. Adam

Schiff asserted investigating a confession of criminal conduct was itself a High Crime or Misdemeanor worthy of impeachment and removal from office – allegedly because it yielded some political advantage over an unannounced political and potential rival.

Remember, Giuliani, compile a dossier that was turned over to the State Department a month before Biden announced his candidacy for an office he had been seeking nomination to since 1988 and he had consistently failed in each attempt. But he also had a long history of representing special interests, and there was the issue of his son's connection to the corruption engaged in by Burisma Holdings.

French investigative journalist Olivier Berruyer reported that President Petro Poroshenko was directly involved in corruption and that Hunter Biden's job at the gas company Burisma was a bribe to his father, the US vice president. The related timeline and interviews with those having firsthand knowledge of the transactions were presented in a documentary series entitled '*UkraineGate: Inconvenient facts.*'

The documentary presents former Deputy Prosecutor-General Renat Kuzmin asserting Hunter Biden was hired *"solely to pressure Ukrainian authorities into stopping the criminal investigations into Burisma."* And his statement fully explains the million dollars a year do-nothing paycheck Hunter received.

Former MP Oleksandr Onyschenko stated, late in 2015, Mykola Zlochevsky used him to relay a $50 million bribe offer to Poroshenko to make the investigations go away – and that the president agreed. The former parliamentarian and close associate of Poroshenko has since turned whistleblower, admitting to taking bribes himself in exchange for votes, such as the one to remove Shokin. This gives us a firsthand assertion of the specific quid pro quo relationship between Burisma's owner and the firing of Prosecutor General Shokin.

Of course, it is necessary to keep in mind that the impeachment was based on the concept that Trump wanted to investigate a political rival. But, given Trump's rise from Reality TV star to Potus, would he feel the need to extort, for political purposes, an investigation into a man who had bragged about committing extortion, and since 1988 failed 3-times to achieve the Democratic presidential nomination – and who was noted for his self-destructive gaffes and his insulting voters while on the campaign trail.

What was being investigated?

Biden had sat in front of an international audience and C-SPAN cameras to BRAG about committing Extortion of Ukraine officials to fire a Prosecutor General – as Biden said, *"I'm leaving in six hours. If the prosecutor is not fired, you're not getting the money."'*

The money was a Billion Dollar guarantee that would back the purchase of weapons and supplies to stop Russia's Ukraine invasion.

This was money Ukraine needed to survive as a free nation. We are told by State Department witnesses that Biden's criminal actions were "Government Policy" and were fully supported by other nations.

If it was government policy, that it follows that it was the policy of President Barack Obama, as confirmed. We also know Hunter Biden was on the board of Burisma Holdings from April 2014 until May 2019. Joseph Cofer Black joined the board in February 2017 – he's a former CIA official who became foreign policy adviser to Mitt Romney's presidential campaign and Romney opposed Trump on one Article in the impeachment.

Note that it was just before Trump asked for MLAT data on the Bidens, the next step after the extensive inquiries Giuliani had been making – it was only then, when Ukraine had an honest President in office, that Hunter exited. Of course, the MLAT consistent request was leveraged by Schiff as his attack on Trump that denied the reality of the basis for request – but, Schiff lies and distorts everything; here he hurt the Biden Ukraine profit center.

Daria Kaleniuk, head of the non-governmental Anti-Corruption Action Center in Kyiv has said, *"I believe the only reason Burisma and Zlochevsky were inviting people with such names was to whitewash their reputation and to present themselves as a company doing legitimate business in Ukraine."*

Whitewashing Burisma necessitates attacking any who would investigate Burisma – and, as the Impeachment showed, Schiff and the Democratic Swamp Denizens attacked Trump for asking about those being paid a million dollars a year to do the whitewashing – their contacts were the brushes being used. In 2012, prosecutorial attacks on Burisma began, Cofer Black joined Romney's presidential campaign as his Foreign Policy and National Security Advisory Team "special adviser." Schiff, Nadler, Jeffries, Lofgren, Garcia, Crow and Demings were fighting to stop investigations into America-Burisma connections by undercutting the Constitutional separation of powers.

As we know, President Obama, who spent twelve-years teaching Constitutional Lawyer (1992-2004) at the University of Chicago Law School, asserted the Presidential right to use "leverage" against other nations – constituting an unchallenged policy President Trump would have every right to continue. But the House Managers apparently were asserting Obama – possibly, Kennedy who utilized it during the Cuban Missile Crisis and other interactions with the then Soviet Union (the Union of Soviet Socialist Republics, subsequently reduced to being just Russia) – should be denied the right to exert leverage to achieve some political or national benefit. Fundamentally, the conflict with Russia is just a political alternative to war.

Russia is in a military conflict with Ukraine, which was cited in my March 2014 publication of: *"Death Over Life: A Prophecy of America's Destruction*, in connection with Russian anti-Semitism: *"In March 2014, the Kremlin has issued more condemnations of anti-Semitism than in the preceding decade; anti-Semitism was on the lips of the Russian Ambassador to the United Nations, their Foreign Minister, and even President Vladimir Putin."*

After the fall of the Soviet Union, restructuring attitudes takes on importance – the Czarist Pale of Settlement territories comprised Lithuania, Latvia, Belarus, Ukraine, and Poland. We hear that anti-Semitism is on the rise, and in *"Jonathon's POTUS Cousins"* I pointed out that, beginning with *"the Immigration Restriction League whose purpose was to address the issue of southern and eastern European immigrants {basically Pale of Settlement Jews} who were considered racially inferior to Anglo-Saxons,"* America declared itself opposed to the people in those regions – because they were Jewish. Even those who were not "Jewish" had Jewish family or ancestors and identified with being victims of "anti-Semitism" sponsored by both America and Russia.

When, in 2014, Obama provided a $53 million aid package that included vehicles, patrol boats, body armor, and night-vision goggles, as well as humanitarian assistance, but rejected Ukrainian President Petro Poroshenko for lethal aid, he sent a subliminal message. Trump is the father of an Orthodox Jew and has twice married immigrants from ancient Eastern European Jewish settlement territories. Trump is reported to have given Ukraine appropriate lethal aid and that has sent a different message.

Biden leveraging loan guarantees to fire what many in Ukraine view as a corruption-fighting Prosectuor General also sent a message.

In March 2016, the Pew Research Center issued a report saying 69% of those supporting Trump's nomination, said immigrants are a burden, while less than 14% of Sanders and less than 17% of Clinton supporters considered immigrants a burden on the country. Thus, if we phrase it in terms of Obama's Fence which became Trump's Wall, Trump entered the race with 69% of GOP and 15% of Democrats on his side. Then add the pro-Israel with Jerusalem as its capital aspect and his subliminal base expands but remains nominal in terms of all voters – where a December 2019 Gallup poll found 28% of Americans identified as Democrat and a similar 28% Republican the immigrants as burden issue has roughly 23.5% of party-affiliated Americans in support of some form of means-testing immigration rules in a culture where Jews are seen as already rich and successful or capable of becoming so; but Latinos and Puerto Ricans are seen as a perpetually stereotypical *"Westside Story"* underclass.

We have issues of aid for Ukraine's survival being held so that a Prosecutor freezing Burisma assets can be fired; the POTUS who, under MLAT seeks to get information on the bragging of endangering Ukraine being impeached because House members decided – without evidence – that investigation might be 'political.' But they also come from states that want illiterate immigrants so they can gerrymander their State population and increase its Representative presence in the House.

Then there is the issue of Ukraine's importance to the Obama-Biden administration and Russian leverage before the Crimea invasion in 2014. For that, we can look back to a pre-election open microphone comment in which President Obama was overheard telling President Dmitri Medvedev of Russia he and Putin would have "more flexibility" to negotiate after the 2012 election.

We the media is presented with an open mic event it is given the opportunity to accidentally eavesdrop on private comments and learns it would not otherwise be privy too. The House Managers were anxious to hear from John Bolton after it was leaked to the New York Times that he had been told by Trump the Ukraine deal was a "quid pro quo." As we know, Bolton and his publisher denied knowledge of the leak or its source. But his book has predicated the fact he has a long history of being in *"The Room Where It Happened."*

When John Bolton, who was George W. Bush's ambassador to the United Nations, heard Obama's comments he called them a *"fire bell in the night."* They inferred Obama would scale back the missile defense program and might yield ground on various national security priorities. Bolton declared: *"There's huge cause for concern..."* and that, because Obama was too much of "a politician to entirely show his hand in the first term, but it would be open season," the truth might come out after his reelection. And maybe – if Obama allowed Russia to move into Crimea and advance on Ukraine – it did.

Historians can ponder that question. What we do know is that Biden was willing to a promise of a Billion Dollars in loan guarantees to threaten Ukraine's survival over the employment of one Prosecutor General employed by a corrupt president. What made Viktor Shokin so critical as to justify allowing Russia to take over Ukraine if he was not removed? And why don't the House Managers want that question answered?

What geopolitical gain did the firing of Shokin offer to Obama and America? We can say a Million Dollars a year is free, do nothing, income might provide advantages to the Biden family; but why would Obama approve it? Did he even know of the extortion, or would he have been told it involved fighting corruption and even then would it be rational to allow a nation to vanish so Russian territory could be expanded to the Polish border?

After the acquittal the media began to cite as an obvious reality: *"no one ever offered a non-corrupt explanation for the Biden family's lucrative entanglement in Ukraine, making the argument much more difficult."*

On 9 February, Author Paul Sperry tweeted: *"Now that the impeachment sham's over, it's up to Sens. Johnson, Graham & Grassley to get to the bottom of who started the Ukraine 'collusion' narrative (after the Russia "collusion" narrative failed), what political bias was involved & how much it was shaped by proven liar Schiff."*

The House lie promoted by Schiff was predicated on solid prior knowledge that Biden would be a candidate and the nominee. It also carried the presumption that other candidates could not hold their own against Biden – who had twice failed to gain the support needed for nomination and had been trying to build a base since 1988.

Setting aside the fact Biden bragged of his crime if Trump was seeking to use a Government Policy action against Biden, he had no leverage over Biden. All Biden needed was to have Former President Barack Obama tweet or call a press conference and declare that he, as

President, did have the policy being conducted and that it included forcing a foreign government to fire its top prosecutor. Biden would, therefore, have been acting properly, and Obama could attest to there being no Burisma linkage.

Where is that affidavit, that certification, that endorsement?

At various times, Mueller, Nadler, Schiff, and others asserted that Trump needed to prove his innocence – it was the argument used when the Senate denied the motion for new witnesses. Trump should come and prove he is innocent. But Biden has a witness – Barack Obama whose Policies those testifying in the House had said were in play when Biden extorted the firing of Shokin.

Obama could have issued such a statement. And yet, he has not. He could not, and cannot because extortion using federal funds is a breach of multiple Federal Laws carrying serious prison time. He is also aware that he did NOT authorize Biden to engage in extortion that would jeopardize the freedom and survival of Ukraine.

Most people know, Obama is a Harvard trained Constitutional Lecturer who would wholeheartedly agree with most points raised by Allan Dershowitz in his Senate arguments. The House Managers and Obama also knew and know, if Obama was called upon to testify – or even issue a statement – on the matter, he would declare Biden did not have authority to make the termination a part the "leverage" and that Adam Schiff was a liar guilty of knowingly misrepresenting the law and the Constitution.

We must note that this does not contradict Obama's 9 February 2015 statement, or the 10 February 2016 GUARDIAN article in which the Washington D.C. based International Monetary Fund [IMF] had affirmed it had warned Ukraine that a $40bn bailout would be halted unless corruption stops.

In 2016, addressing the issue in her IMF role, Christine Lagarde said: *"I am concerned about Ukraine's slow progress in improving governance and fighting corruption, and reducing the influence of vested interests in policymaking."* At the time, she was 'Managing Director of the International Monetary Fund,' and since November 2019 she has been 'President of the European Central Bank,' which means she had firsthand knowledge of both policy and many events. It is in that context she stated: *"Without a substantial new effort to invigorate governance reforms and fight corruption, it is hard to see how the IMF-supported programme can continue and be successful.*

Ukraine risks a return to the pattern of failed economic policies that has plagued its recent history. It is vital that Ukraine's leadership acts now to put the country back on a promising path of reform."

Many have used her words as an attack on Shokin, but we know the *"governance"* was that of the corrupt President and Parliament, as well as the systemic corruption that defined all branches of Ukraine bureaucracy before and after Shokin – but, as UkraineGate has shown, not including Shokin.

It can't be emphasized too much: Obama must defend Biden's extortion of Ukraine to fire Shokin or, by his silence, he validates the fact that those handling the House impeachment propaganda process lied – they were promoting their variation on *"The Emperor's New Clothes"* and counting on their base to see what did not exist.

'*The Emperor's New Clothes*' and '*the elephant in the room*' are '*two sides of the same coin*' – both define characteristics of human perception. With the former, you are to see that which is obviously not there; with the latter, you refuse to see that which is obviously there.

When playing with the 'lawyer's lie', the con artist is continually flipping the coin and takes a position that whatever side is up is really the opposite side. As a result, there is never any truth apart from what they designate to be true. This is guided by their use of buzz words that have no evidence to support them.

The basis is a propaganda rule or law attributed to Nazi Joseph Goebbels: *"Repeat a lie often enough and it becomes the truth."* This is the only law strictly followed by Schiff and the House Managers. In the world of psychologists, this known as the *"illusion of truth"* effect and is one of many techniques of persuasion.

In an honest prosecution, the first step would be to remove any doubt about Biden's innocence, to highlight Trump's guilt. But Biden had bragged of his guilt, of the illegal *quid pro quo*, so they imposed a variation on a traditional *"blame the victim"* mode of attack – accuse Trump of the *quid pro quo* act Biden committed and bragged about. It becomes '*the elephant in the room*' attributed to something other than what it is, to explain the space it occupies – it's a psychologically flipped coin.

Trump is given the power of precognition so that he creates a "scheme" based on knowing Biden would run, become the nominee, and therefore would be the threat replacing Warren and Sanders.

A mystical *quid pro quo* Ukraine did not know existed.

A team of Vanderbilt University psychologists led by Lisa Fazio tested the interaction between an *illusion of truth effect* and prior knowledge of a fact. They paired true and untrue statements, which were divided according to a probability their test subjects would know the truth, and discovered the *illusion of truth effect* was equally strong for known and unknown items – which showed that prior knowledge won't prevent repetition from swaying our judgment of plausibility.

If you want to see how the House Managers used this *Big Lie* technique you need only read the Senate transcripts of house manager statements available, by date and hearing, on the government website

https://www.congress.gov/congressional-record

Without Obama voicing a policy defense, the implication must be that the policy assertion is a lie propagated by Biden and Schiff. If that defense is a lie, then Burisma and the brag become a legitimate area of investigation. On 4 February, Senator Susan Collins of Maine said: *"The president's call was wrong. He should not have mentioned Joe Biden in it, despite his overall concern about corruption in Ukraine. The President of the United States should not be asking a foreign country to investigate a political rival. That is just improper. It was far from a perfect call."*

As I've pointed out, that argument hinges on Joe Biden actually being a political rival at the time of the call. However, historically, it is clear that Biden has over 40-years of failed attempts to achieve high office. In contrast, Trump formally announced his candidacy on 16 June 2015; we know he faced opposition from experienced politicians; 13-months later, on 19 July 2016 he became the Republican nominee – and 3-months after that he was President-elect. Why would he fear Biden?

Was there any rational basis or argument that would make Joe Biden, who had no organized base or campaign team, a threat in a race that had Bernie Sanders-backed by AOC and his 2016 organization?

Senator Collins' talking point relies on accepting the nonsense put forth bu Adam Schiff and because he did not defend Biden, denied by Barack Obama.

Comically, Adam Schiff would assert, *"The timing is driven by the urgency."* And clearly, the only urgency associated with the matter was that Obama did not make himself complicit in the Federal crimes Biden bragged he had committed as Vice President...crimes that where High Crimes if they were crimes. And they do not need to be Federal crimes within the United States, the Shokin complaint in Ukraine is a felony involving the misuse of Biden's Office – that constitutes a High Crime within the Constitutionally related definition.

On 4 February, Senator Susan Collins (R-ME) stated, "*I do not believe that the House has met its burden of showing that the president's conduct, however flawed, warrants the extreme step of immediate removal from office. It is my judgment that except when extraordinary circumstances require a different result, we should entrust to the people the most fundamental decision of a democracy — namely who should lead their country.*"

Schiff is an expert at propagating the *illusion of truth effect* and it makes him a fantastic dishonest prosecutor who habitually asserts "*Lawyer's Lies*" whenever he opens his mouth – outflows a wave of Hyperbole, obfuscation, or verbal distraction couched as hypothetical analogy having no real connection to the reality at hand.

These are the tools of the professional liar turned lawyer. The analysis or explanation of all the instances seen throughout the House and Senate Impeach proceedings would easily fill a book on how to convict innocent defendants. But, the same study is generalized when psychologists deal with the *illusion of truth* or when we reference the elephant in the room and Emperor's magical new clothes.

In his closing statement, Schiff asserted, "*We have proven our case.*" Of course, the question is, "*What Case?*" What did they prove? That Trump spoke to Ukraine; that Biden bragged about extortion to have a prosecutor fired – a prosecutor who apparently was freezing the assets of his son's boss and therefore freezing both justification and source of his son's unearned income?

Schiff ranted on about how "*We have proven Donald Trump guilty, now do impartial justice and convict him. ... History will not be kind to Donald Trump. If you find that the House has proved its case and still vote to acquit, your name will be tied to him with a cord of steel and for all of history.*"

But there is no crime, and history does not normally denigrate those who complied with the moral and ethical laws of their nation.

Following a conventional tactic, Schiff pointed at Trump then described himself and fellow Swamp Denizens: "*He has not changed. He will not change. The plot goes on, the scheming persists, and the danger will never recede.*"

But what "plot"; what "scheme"; what undefined crime is there?

Focus on the "Lawyer's Lies" which FakeNews networks grasp as the basis of their attacks and misrepresentations. We saw one on 3 February 2020 during the Senate summations.

At that time, Schiff provided us with a "Lawyer's Lie" when, on 3 February, he stated: *"Presidents may abuse their power with impunity, they argued. Abuse of power is not a constitutional crime, they claimed. Only statutory crime is a constitutional crime, even though there were no statutory crimes when the Constitution was adopted."*

True but a lie complained of by "Captain Jack Sparrow" – they didn't have any United States statutory crimes, because there was no Constitution or nation. Instead, as the SCOTUS often recognizes, they had English Statutory Law which was what they had in mind when the wrote *"High Crimes and misdemeanors"* as the standard. Schiff lied by telling the truth – and did so dramatically.

If we went by his logic and assertion, the colonists would have had no laws in mind when they wrote their constitutional articles – it means they had no laws defining bribery, treason, murder, theft, or anything else ... Schiff said there were no statutory laws. And isn't it comical that commentators on CNN were quick to accept the Colonies were lawless territories? Or, maybe, they believed the 613 Biblical laws were strictly followed and constituted the basis of definition for High Crimes.

CNN commentators point to Clinton being apologetic after his acquittal, while and Trump wasn't. But Clinton engaged in adultery of sorts – Oral in the Oval with an intern – and denied *"sexual relations with that woman."* Trump enforced the laws of the nation and was compliant with MLAT data management requirements. And, after the Trial, as the CNN commentators were making their false comparisons, Ukraine's justice system was considering a felony violation complaint against former Vice President Joseph R. Biden.

On Saturday, 1 February, Senator Lamar Alexander Tweeted a fifteen part explanation for his Friday vote to deny more witnesses or testimony and acknowledged so things were "inappropriate":

I worked with other senators to make sure that we have the right to ask for more documents and witnesses, but there is no need for more evidence to prove something that has already been proven and that does not meet the U.S. Constitution's high bar for an impeachable offense.1/15

There is no need for more evidence to prove that the president asked Ukraine to investigate Joe Biden and his son, Hunter; he said this on television on October 3, 2019, and during his July 25, 2019, telephone call with the president of Ukraine. 2/15

There is no need for more evidence to conclude that the president withheld United States aid, at least in part, to pressure Ukraine to investigate the Bidens; the House managers have proved this with what they call a "mountain of overwhelming evidence." 3/15

There is no need to consider further the frivolous second article of impeachment that would remove the president for asserting his constitutional prerogative to protect confidential conversations with his close advisers. 4/15

But the Constitution does not give the Senate the power to remove the president from office and ban him from this year's ballot simply for actions that are inappropriate. 7/15

The question then is not whether the president did it, but whether the United States Senate or the American people should decide what to do about what he did. 8/15

I believe that the Constitution provides that the people should make that decision in the presidential election that begins in Iowa on Monday. 9/15

The Senate has spent nine long days considering this "mountain" of evidence, the arguments of the House managers and the president's lawyers, their answers to senators' questions and the House record. 10/15

Even if the House charges were true, they do not meet the Constitution's "treason, bribery, or other high crimes and misdemeanors" standard for an impeachable offense. 11/15

The framers believed that there should never, ever be a partisan impeachment. ... Yet not one House Republican voted for these articles. 12/15

It would create the weapon of perpetual impeachment to be used against future presidents whenever the House of Representatives is of a different political party. 14/15

Our founding documents provide for duly elected presidents who serve with "the consent of the governed," not at the pleasure of the United States Congress. Let the people decide. 15/15

CHAPTER SEVEN – SOTU 2020

"Sometimes I reflect, you know, is there something else I could do to make ... some of the House [Republican] caucus members not — not paint horns on my head?" ~ Barack Obama, 1 March 2013

Ancient Stonehenge had 56-stones and the fifty-seventh is the first of the next cycle; a POTUS term is four years, times 56 yields 224 years; that cycle finishes when four multiplied by 57. George Washington was inaugurated on 30 April 1789, at Federal Hall in New York; 224 years later would be 1 May 2013, and the next exact cycle began 1 May 2017. But America changed its inauguration dates so we are stuck with 20 January 2013 and 2017.

For the mystics and superstitious America has begun its second cycle and that is marked by the Inauguration of Donald John Trump; as those who read JPC know that the end of the first cycle ended with the 2nd inauguration of George Washington's tenth cousin; we know Washington took office when Africans were American slaves, they then became African-American and at the end of the cycle the nation saw a true African+American in the Oval Office. We can declare that to have been the true State of the Union in the final years of the Original Great Experiment.

As this is being written we are three years into the first phase of the 2nd "mystical henge" cycle of America's history. How do we define it, and ourselves, in the annals of history?

What is the State of the Union when the President can be impeached without committing a crime; when he follows the policies of previous presidents and obeys the "treaty" law to explore the truth behind a former high official of the United States entertaining an international audience with his boast or brag extorting, coercing, or blackmailing a foreign head of state into firing his chief prosecutor?

Granted, we think in strange ways and accept strange things. In 1968, Erich von Däniken produced a fantasy entitled *"Chariots of the Gods"* – the premise being that our forebearers were idiots and could not possibly have created monolithic structures like Stonehenge or the Great Pyramids. As with the works of French author Robert Charroux, von Däniken followed an ancient astronaut theme in which alien receive credit for the intelligence and skills of Indo-Europeans. In both *"Grandpa Was a Deity"* and *"Genesis of*

Genesis" yDNA, math, and shared elements of common mythology allow those who respect rather than denigrate their ancestral roots to have an accurate understanding of the modern civilization's roots.

This is relevant only because of the significance of the cycles throughout history. The 56 is three 18s, and 57 three 19s, and all have astrological significance in modern and ancient world terms – Stonehenge has 56 upright stones and nineteen is a common divisor associated with the lifespan of the Biblical patriarchs. If we talk of ancient generations, again nineteen years is applicable.

There is a factual logic in some contexts but no apparent logic in others – yet it works. We can speak in terms of periods of eighteen or Nineteen; the fun begins when it's applied to American Presidential terms.

Consider 18-terms or 72 years; we have 1861, the civil war and end of slavery; 19-terms 1865 the war's end. Washington was inaugurated in April; the Civil War 12 April 1861 – 9 April 1865.

Repeat the process to reach 12 April 1933: Reich Statistical Office Director Friedrich Bürgdorfer announced a census that would every Jew and non-Aryan in the nation. Then, on 9 April 1937, the Kamikaze became the first Japanese-built aircraft to fly from Japan to Europe – of course, *"Kamikaze"* would take on a different meaning to be a suicidal aircraft crashing into an enemy target. But properly, its meaning is that of a "divine wind" and providential storm sent by the gods to protect their supplicants.

Trump evidences the *"Kamikaze"* or *"divine wind"* character whose cycle is tied to January 1941 and the third inauguration of Franklin D. Roosevelt. Traits invoking Impeachment for winning an election via the Electoral College, following the law, and being a PC.

For those who believe in such things, this might represent some form of spiritual connection denoting points of change – is it violent or simply change? Maybe it's as imaginary as von Däniken's aliens as the source of human magnificence. Certainly, humans are incapable of anything meaningful or mutually beneficial.

We've entered the second cycle of American national history. The nation formally began in April 1789, but the battle for its creation is dated between 19 April 1775 and 3 September 1783. If we apply the cycle to the war, on 9 April 2003 Baghdad fell to U.S. forces, and on 14 September 2011, Elizabeth Warren announced her intention to run to become a Massachusetts Senator; Revolution to inauguration, under five years, so five years later found Warren running for President.

In terms of cycles, the State of the Union is in transition. It had achieved the 58th quadrennial period in American history. In terms of politics, transitional periods are generally a mess. And it would be hard to argue that the House Managers and Speaker of the House haven't worked rather hard at making things messier than they needed to be.

We just looked at stupid patterns or cycles, pulled from thin air, to define "the pulse of a nation" and it's beginning a new journey through history. This is a period transitioning along a path defined by Democratic-Socialism and taking the form of Bernie Sanders or AOC. Sanders ran in 2016, he's not a POTUS Cousin and therefore would be a dramatic shift if nominated and then elected. And he must overcome the propaganda training of McCarthyism which made a connection between Socialist and Communist.

On 9 January he stated '*Obviously I am not a communist.*' He also added a possibility that Trump '*doesn't know the difference*' between Socialism and Communism. But the average American has no idea that there is a difference – nor do they understand that the Scandinavian countries were Socialist in the days of the Vikings and that Jesus was a Socialist who praised as an ideal the Samaritan who provided free healthcare, along with free food and shelter while he recovered – and he did not inquire about the man's finances or care that he was a wealthy merchant.

Karl Marx is seen as the inventor of socialism. But, given the reality of his origins, he was just making non-denomination the Biblical teachings which had merchants support scholars and their families, or held that give to others what we would want if we were in their place, or do not do to them what we would not accept if in their place. Marx could be seen as a supporter of capitalism – his whole economic concept was based on the use of "surplus capital."

The State of the Union is that we are moving into the era of Star Trek and a Federation where everyone has the basics of life and then follow their interests and loves because they don't need to be concerned with "making a living."

Of course, readers of this series and its associated books are well aware of the difference that is cited where Marx is mentioned in JPC. Those who oppose the teachings of Jesus are the first to oppose Medicare for All [M4A]; those who support his teachings demand it, as would anyone who understands that the Hebrew scriptures promote and encourage things that benefit all and constitute the solid economics of success that have made Jews hated by those locked into the economics of poverty, or who were the masters keeping the peasants locked into poverty and slavery.

But isn't that exactly what the anti-Constitutionalists – who are posing as *Dump Trumpers* – are behaving irrationally. Lawyers Lies work on normal jurors but, speaking in the senate, they were being used in lawyers who knew how to recognize those lies. As a result, there was a politically partisan vote to convict targeting the gullible among the Democratic base while alienating the intelligent.

The result was increased post-trial support for Trump – as for any alleged facts, during the 3 February summation, White House Deputy Counsel Mike Purpura pointed out that the House's evidence and President Zelensky refuted their false correlation:

"First, the President did not condition security assistance or a meeting on anything during the July 25 call. In fact, both Ambassador Yovanovitch and Mr. Tim Morrison confirmed that the Javelin missiles and the security assistance were completely unrelated. ...

"Second, President Zelensky and his top advisers agreed that there was nothing wrong with the July 25 call and that they felt no pressure from President Trump. President Zelensky said that the call was ``good," ``normal," and ``no [one] pushed me.' ...

"Third, President Zelensky and the highest levels of the Ukrainian Government did not learn of the pause until August 28, 2019--more than a month after the July 25 call between President Trump and President Zelensky."

When it was his turn, Adam Schiff repeated his lie about overwhelming evidence and proof of guilt – but without mention of what Trump was guilty of. He then ignored the presented facts and again asserted for his gullible base:

"The House has proven the President's guilt. He tried to coerce an ally into helping him cheat by smearing his opponent. He betrayed our national security in order to do it when he withheld military aid to our ally and violated the law to do so."

Schiff denied and dismissed three points of documented fact so he could perpetuate his pattern of lies. And Americans blindly accepted what Schiff and media outlets like CNN said they must-see. The magical wardrobe the phony tailor assured the Emperor only the wise could see – those who were fools they saw it.

But worse, it was the media who promoted the "tailor's con-job."

They had no interest in the survival of the nation – *if it bleeds it leads* and if there is no blood, find or create a victim and cut them. When the State of the Nation in the period of major change which would determine its future and possibly that of a world already in a state of major [climate] change, having a media antagonistic those things needed to ensure national survival does not help.

Change is interesting, a technological difference can change both routine behavior and language. The Impeachment-Climate cycles came together at the beginning of the 58th quadrennial and made the "existential threat" concept meaningful – existence being redefined but human activities. This made "existential" the defining buzzword for 2020, a year when all things posed seemed to present a threat to humanity.

Jim Messina, Obama's campaign manager in 2012, stated in a Financial Times op-ed: *"I believe that the re-election of Donald Trump would pose an existential threat to the U.S. and the world. The next eight-and-a-half exhilarating, frustrating and exhausting months will determine the course of history."* {10 February}

And he was correct. The events of the new century are, to the extent that the United States can influence them, is determined by American voters and self-centered media. As history will note in the context of his facilitating the long-desired Impeachment, Biden can be seen as an existential threat to a functional government. His nomination and election would return the swamp denizens to their former positions of power. Propaganda is central to the process.

With the creation or emergence of the Internet came instant communication that incorporated video and auto-recording, while also allowing archiving and retrieval with the added benefit of wide-ranging search capabilities use Google, Bing, Yahoo, and other search engines. This allows the characteristics of classic propaganda or persuasion to be exercised on a wider audience, but it also allows their audience to more quickly learn how to identify those tactics.

As we have seen, Schiff and his fellow lawyer politicians rely upon *the illusion of truth effect* they would normally use before a jury. The same tactic has been utilized by persuasive orators since the days of ancient Greece and Rome. We can even go back 6,000 years to the dawn of the Indus Valley civilization and it's use in the religious context still effective today.

An example is found in the assertion "*Grandpa Was A Deity*" which was put forward as an assertion of tribal identity derived from being descendants of a child of God and a mortal. In the Bible, it is acknowledged in the Flood story prelude – descendants of the sons of God are identified as '*men of renown*'. In India, the Chenchu tribe derives their special or sacred status from the same claim used to describe the origin of Hercules; in Christianity ascribed to Jesus, but taken a notch higher, as the child of the supreme deity.

Concepts that resonate and hold a traditional status are used as the platform for religions, con artists, or those whose power is derived from persuasion. Each used the *illusion of truth* effect, and we commonly accept or welcome it as a source of comfort. However, we are now in an era where the comfort of tradition is what provides the existential threat. And accepted buzzwords trigger belief in the most ridiculous things – such as the use of the words "Fact Check" in a FaceBook post that announced: "*FACT CHECK: Yes, Nancy Pelosi Moved Billions from SSI to Cover Impeachment Costs.*"

There were people who accepted the impeachment process had cost Billions of dollars, and that Pelosi could raid Social Security to cover the cost.

Speaking of Pelosi, she lacks the skills to utilize the lawyer's lies, so the cameras catch her using body language as her means of expressing emotion and entering a degree of control.

During the State of the Union speech on 7 February 2019, Pelosi displayed her disdain for Trump through the use of the "*seal flipper clap*" – arms straight out, wrists turned so hands are parallel to the floor. On 4 February, the SOTU address was the day before the impeachment verdict which Pelosi knew was destined to be an acquittal. When President Trump concluded, her comment was expressed by tearing up or shredding her copy of his speech.

It was a childish temper tantrum destruction type of display.

Later, she would be asked about her childish display, and she said, "*I tore up a manifesto of mistruths. ... I don't need any lessons from anybody, especially the president of the United States, about dignity. Dignity. Is it okay to start saying four more years in the House of Representatives? It's just unheard of."*

Her piqued ire clearly showing in her words, she took a lead from Schiff and lied through the phrasing of her description of the SOTU speech she had previously prepared for easy destruction – *"a manifesto of mistruths"* that was a boilerplate speech.

Pelosi demonstrated characteristics stereotypically presented in period movies as prime and proper upper-class wannabe ladies who generally show their "good manners" in a manner weaponized by their tone and body language. Consistent with the stereotype, when such "ladies" open their mouth venom politely pours forth – Speaker Pelosi is classic, as stated by her daughter who said *'She'll cut your head off'*.

As mentioned throughout this book series, Trump's style is derived from Queens or NYC techniques. These would include the bestowing nicknames as a variation on schoolyard name-calling, or the playing with names – as when Sen. Joe Manchin (D-W.Va.) was dubbed *"munchkin."*

Of course, it got the type of response Trump enjoys – on 10 February, Manchin retaliation was telling MSNBC: *"Do you think names bother me? Do I look like I'm small and fragile? Names don't bother me and the president knows he can't get to me that way. He can call me all the names he wants to, it makes him look like an immature adult. And I hope he rises above that, I really would. I think it's best for our country."*

Immaturity is an interesting concept in a context where those children in the House of Representatives have been throwing temper tantrums every since the Constitution did its job and the Electoral College chose a descendant of the 4-Sisters over an outsider. Pelosi can call the SOTU speech a *"manifesto of mistruths,"* and later she can try to justify her childishness by making her actions symbolic: *"He shredded the truth, so I shredded his speech. ...What we heard last night was a disgrace."*

Let's look at the basic boilerplate SOTU Trump delivered. It had the obligatory acknowledgments of individuals in the balcony and there was the Medal of Freedom for Rush Limbaugh...WHY?

It was the last State of the Union message before the election, the acquittal final verdict would be the next day, and the President began with what is his favorite technique – being positive: *"Three years ago, we launched the great American comeback. Tonight, I stand before you to share the incredible results. Jobs are booming, incomes are soaring, poverty is plummeting, crime is falling, confidence is surging, and our country is thriving and highly respected again."*

American media thrives on being negative, seeing the worst in everything, and offering nothing to improve things. Elizabeth Warren said she had a plan, and then demonstrates an inability to plan a caucus or primary campaign good enough to surpass Bernie Sanders or Pete Buttigieg – even Senator Amy Klobuchar surpassed Warren in the first to delegate states.

In New Hampshire, Buttigieg and Sanders received 23-29% more than Klobuchar; Klobuchar received 114% more than Warren. But neither Sanders nor Klobuchar is a Potus Cousin; they have no connection to the 4-Sisters and if tradition is to hold, they cannot occupy the Oval Office. In terms of that kinship, Warren is equal to Trump; but, what she gains in the formal knowledge of the law she loses in its application within a global economic environment.

With his opening, Trump presented the true current reality of the demographic-economic environment which engaged when the first of the Baby-Boomers turned 62 in 2007. In 2021, those born in 1955 will be moving onto the Social Security rolls, which will keep the economy going – unless the President and Congress take actions necessary to destroy it. The 2020 census will reveal the economic possibilities, by revealing how many Baby-Boomers are alive; in any event, the economy can stay strong and growing through 2025, so Trump's opening words should remain truthful and repeatable. But, Pelosi doesn't want it to be true, and, being 80-years-old in a nation where the life expectancy is 79 years and 11 months, wasn't likely to be around that long – in February, she'd already reached the average expiration date.

America was coming back from the demographic transition it saw as the Great Recession that was created by Reaganomics and Bush-43.

Reagan, utilizing Reaganomics, created a situation that would see the American economy implode when the majority of Baby-Boomers died – around 2035. Combined with other cycles and forces, this would set the stage for global war in 2033/5.

Trump then said: *"The years of economic decay are over. The days of our country being used, taken advantage of, and even scorned by other nations are long behind us. Gone, too, are the broken promises, jobless recoveries, tired platitudes and constant excuses for the depletion of American wealth, power and prestige."*

Was this declaration of positivity a lie or some *"manifesto of mistruth"* that we should denounce?

Trump told the joint session of Congress: *"In just three short years, we have shattered the mentality of American decline, and we have rejected the downsizing of America's destiny. We have totally rejected the downsizing. We are moving forward at a pace that was unimaginable just a short time ago, and we are never, ever going back."*

In their private lives, elderly Americans were downsizing. In their economic lives, downsizing had defined the practice known as outsourcing. But Trump was actively seeking to repatriate all those industries lost to China, India, and other poor developing nations.

Trump went on to be positive, But, as she stated, Pelosi had wanted it to be a lie – she wanted everything to be negative, even as the financial markets were recording record highs. However, what we are seeing is a disinformation campaign abetted by various media outlets which could, rightfully, in the modern internet era be termed *"FakeNews outlets."* Pelosi, among other members of the House, is aiding and abetting illicit actors of the type represented in Crimea-Russian operations being well documented in research published in places such as the "Journal of Information Warfare."

She didn't like the fact Trump declared: *"I say to the people of our great country and to the members of Congress: The state of our Union is stronger than ever before."* And other Dump Trump people seem to have the same problem. They offer nothing positive.

On 11 February Politico reported Nancy Pelosi pivoting from the attempts to invent grounds for impeachment and beginning to seek ways to justify declaring the economy a failure. The article stated, *"Pelosi hosted a special speaker's meeting on [11 February] with a top Obama economics adviser to explain to Democrats why the economy isn't actually as strong as Trump claims and how they can message that to voters."*

Trump's SOTU speech brushed across critical voter concerns of education, health care, and the economy that are core Progressive issues. The economy is doing well and on a broader scale, the nation saw Ivanka Trump making real progress with the Women's Global Development and Prosperity Initiative (W-GDP) which, in its first year, helped lift 12 million woman and their economies.

The concept is related to raising the Minimum Wage. When women are empowered economically, their newly acquired wealth is reinvested families and community; the same thing happens when workers or those on Social Security no longer need welfare subsidies to survive.

We should note, the House did pass an increased Minimum Wage bill early in 2019, the same bill was presented to the Senate by Bernie Sanders but never came to a vote because the impeachment disrupted the process; having entered the campaign season, a vote on it would carry political implications. But it doesn't matter. The legislation raises the Federal minimum over a six-year, denying the nation a developed economic foundation it will need in 2025.

W-GDP is an international initiative whose goal is to elevate 50 million women in the developing world by 2025 – which could place those nations on a par with the United States by 2035. There is bipartisan support for its goals, funding, and management under U.S. Agency for International Development Administrator (USAID) to reach 22 countries. The only restriction is to ensure there is no similar benefit domestically – which is what makes the Sanders and Warren campaign so interesting.

However, domestically, Trump's SOTU message pointed out: *"The unemployment rate for women reached the lowest level in almost 70 years. And, last year, women filled 72 percent of all new jobs added."* Which, we can presume, is part of Pelosi's *"manifesto of mistruths"* to which we might add, *"The veterans unemployment rate dropped to a record low. The unemployment rate for disabled Americans has reached an all-time low."*

Trump said, *"This is a blue-collar boom."*

Pelosi's response was to establish a propaganda network to deny the achievements Trump claimed, even as he was taking steps to support veterans and military spouses by signing the Supporting Veterans in STEM Careers Act, which he said, *"directs the National Science Foundation to work with other federal agencies to expand veteran eligibility for STEM-related programs and encourages veteran participation in these critical fields.".*

Accompanying the Veterans initiative, Trump also instituted the VA Mission Act which is effectively a step toward *Medicaid for All* because it allows veterans to find and utilize the best healthcare options available – be that at VA facilities or community providers.

Veterans, Medicare and Medicaid retiree recipients comprise the major healthcare demographic in the nation; with them covered, those receiving government funding fall into a common basket.

Medicaid for All (M4A) requires overlapping bureaucracies to be unified or simplified; once that has been achieved, the majority of the population would fall within the system – making expansion of that system a minor demographic adjustment.

Just one day before he would be acquitted, Trump was telling the world, "*Since my election, U.S. stock markets have soared 70 percent, adding more than $12 trillion to our nation's wealth, transcending anything anyone believed was possible. This is a record. It is something that every country in the world is looking up to. They admire. Consumer confidence has just reached amazing new highs.*"

As I've pointed out, each modern impeachment or credible threat has resulted in a decline in the financial markets. Pelosi's effort didn't phase the markets, allowing Trump to announce: *Since my election, U.S. stock markets have soared 70 percent, adding more than $12 trillion to our nation's wealth, transcending anything anyone believed was possible. This is a record. It is something that every country in the world is looking up to. They admire. Consumer confidence has just reached amazing new highs.*"

Yet, consistent with the impeachment, refuting the objective evidence, Pelosi and the House Managers, held to their "*manifesto of mistruths*" scenario, knowing full well their legion of believers would accept anything which refutes the evidence of their own eyes.

Still, Trump had to attack a cornerstone of the Sanders and Warren platform, so he said: "*One hundred thirty-two lawmakers in this room have endorsed legislation to impose a socialist takeover of our health care system, wiping out the private health insurance plans of 180 million very happy Americans. To those watching at home tonight, I want you to know: We will never let socialism destroy American health care.*"

There is no socialist attack on healthcare. M4A is the medical care system we already have but have yet to expand universally – and when it is, costs will drop sharply. Privatized healthcare is not healthcare at all. It is a system where private companies take your money and then hire people to find excuses not to pay claims, while also making the deductibles so high that they seldom need to pay for real medical needs.

His premise was a form of Lawyers Lie. But he then went on to say what he was targeting: *"Over 130 legislators in this chamber have endorsed legislation that would bankrupt our nation by providing free taxpayer-funded health care to millions of illegal aliens, forcing taxpayers to subsidize free care for anyone in the world who unlawfully crosses our borders."*

In the first Democratic Debate, all those on the stage raised their hands in agreement with the question of providing free that healthcare to illegals – even as American citizens were being denied it. But on 4 May 2017, Trump praised Australia's healthcare system, which Bernie Sanders pointed out consisted of a blend of both public and private markets, in which a publicly funded universal healthcare system was integrated into a system of medical services provided by the private sector. This means Trump and Sanders were talking about the same system – but focusing on different aspects.

Sanders would say, *"Thank you, Mr. President. Let us move to a Medicare-for-all system that does what every other major country on earth does — guarantee healthcare to all people at a fraction of the cost per capita that we spend. Thank you, Mr. President. We'll quote you on the floor of the Senate."*

While everyone seems to agree the nation needs healthcare consistent all other industrialized nations, the context is different. America can do better and Trump's ego embodies elements seen in Melania Trump's BE BEST children's well-being initiative – or maybe her program reflects her husband's approach to life and his drive for success. One thing is sure, Trump would want a healthcare program his grandchildren could praise to their children.

So we wonder at the *"mistruth"* underlying his claim to have taken on the big pharmaceutical companies. With the result that he was able to tell his audience:

"We have approved a record number of affordable generic drugs, and medicines are being approved by the F.D.A. at a

faster clip than ever before. And I was pleased to announce last year that, for the first time in 51 years, the cost of prescription drugs actually went down.

"And working together, Congress can reduce drug prices substantially from current levels. I've been speaking to Senator Chuck Grassley of Iowa and others in Congress in order to get something on drug pricing done, and done quickly and properly. I'm calling for bipartisan legislation that achieves the goal of dramatically lowering prescription drug prices. Get a bill on my desk, and I will sign it into law immediately."

When Trump concluded his State of the Union, he again drew on positive boilerplate pronouncements Pelosi believed untrue and certainly worthy of being torn to shreds.

"This is our glorious and magnificent inheritance. We are Americans. We are pioneers. We are the pathfinders. We settled the New World, we built the modern world, and we changed history forever by embracing the eternal truth that everyone is made equal by the hand of Almighty God.

"America is the place where anything can happen. America is the place where anyone can rise. And here, on this land, on this soil, on this continent, the most incredible dreams come true.

"This nation is our canvas, and this country is our masterpiece. We look at tomorrow and see unlimited frontiers just waiting to be explored. Our brightest discoveries are not yet known. "Our most thrilling stories are not yet told. Our grandest journeys are not yet made. The American Age, the American Epic, the American adventure has only just begun.

"Our spirit is still young, the sun is still rising, God's grace is still shining, and, my fellow Americans, the best is yet to come.

"Thank you..."

With that "Thank you" the nation once again resumed that change of cycle conflict which would determine its survival. Not as a nation, but as a nation of importance. This same determination was being made in Britain, where BREXIT yelled they would "go-it-alone" while also debating the continued role of the monarchy.

SIDE THOUGHTS

Much of the Western World – and America in particular – is of an evolutionary nature manifesting in a passive aggressive culture that will accept self-harm as a premise for depriving others of those things which ultimately benefit all.

There must be a reason we deny a Universal Basic Income to ourselves and others. We all know that, if we had one, we would not need to have Social Security or Public Assistance (Welfare), or even unemployment insurance.

If we had a UBI system, the trillion or so Congress is debating as a Wuhan virus countermeasure stimulus would not be necessary.

It is true, UBI might mean some people might not "work", but they might still be productive.

During the Renaissance, many of the creative greats survived due to "benefactors" and "Patrons" who supported them and their work. I often refer to the Biblical Tribal Structure where merchants supported scholars and their families – isn't that what created the much hated Jewish mercantile tradition anti-Semites denounce and we see in classic "The Merchant of Venice"?

Why not have "Medicare for All"? Isn't that what has been invoked to respond to the medical needs created by COVID-19, the Wuhan Coronavirus? Why not make it permanent and thus be ready when the next and far worse pandemic emerges about a decade from now – in the 2030s?

The Nigerian novelist, Chinua Achebe, is often quoted: "*He who will hold another down in the mud must stay in the mud to keep him down.*"

It is a byproduct of the passive aggressive approach, we harm ourselves using the excuse that we are stopping others from harming us through their "freeloading." But, the clear fact remains, we are the ones who are really being harmed. It's the flip-side of "*Do unto others as you would have them done unto you.*" Or, "*Whatever you do to others will be done to you.*"

People hate Trump because he realizes the reality of this and so will praise people in the hope that their reaction will come back as deserving of that praise. His detractors seek the worst outcome, and so experience that which they are effectively asking for.

Coincidently, those who attack Trump the most represent the states subsequently being hardest hit by the Wuhan Coronavirus.

CHAPTER EIGHT – VERDICT

"Every individual necessarily labors to render the annual revenue of society as great as he can. He generally neither intends to promote the public interest nor knows how much he is promoting it. He intends only his own gain, and he is, in this, as in many other cases, led by an invisible hand to promote an end which was not part of his intention." ~ Adam Smith

As anticipated throughout the Impeachment, on 5 January the Senate acquitted President Trump of both *Abuse of Power* and *Obstruction of Congress* – 52:48 and 53:47, where a supra-majority of 33:67 was needed to convict, remove Trump, and elevate Michael Richard Pence to the Oval Office as POTUS-46.

The fact that the move to impeach was not based on facts, or any actual misconduct or crime, points us in the direction of wanting Mike Pence to be the President. When this was raised in 2017, the response was that they would then impeach him, which would mean the Speaker of the House of Representatives, Nancy Pelosi, would become President – or POTUS-47 – without ever having run for the office.

But that's a very convoluted Machiavellian conspiracy theory and buried in context of logical contradiction often seen in the world of the *Lawyer's Lie*. As Senate Majority Leader Mitch McConnell (R-Ky) viewed it, he was perplexed by the inherent dichotomy that was created by an assertion the evidence against Trump was obvious and overwhelming, yet needed additional documentary evidence or witness testimony.

McConnell said, *"This was a political loser for [Democrats] ... in the short-term, this has been a colossal political mistake."*

Originally, Pelosi had tried to avoid what was just a *"political exercise"* in undermining the Constitution and economy. But it did achieve something – it served to clearly identified various Swamp Denizens and their devoted followers. Plus, psychologists will enjoy benefits of clear and pervasive proof that *"The Emperor's New Clothes"* was a timeless story of the way the human need to see that which they believe they should be seeing will override the evidence before their own eyes, and the very basic logic they need to survive.

The verdict is in. A sizable percentage of people are morons.

Worse, what was deemed a joke, in the film *Blazing Saddles* – *"You've got to remember that these are just simple farmers. These are people of the land. The common clay of the new West. You know... morons."* – describes those nurtured by propagandists seeking to disrupt American Democracy.

Of course, historians might look back and laugh about how things work out. A year earlier (11 October 2018) Attorney Michael Avenatti tweeted *"Donald Trump Jr. Would be indicted before his birthday on 12-31-18. If you doubt my prediction, please check my record over the past 7 months."*

A year later Avenatti had been indicted, and on St Valentine's Day 2020, a New York Federal Court jury found him guilty on three counts related to attempted extortion of Nike athletic apparel; he still faced charges for stealing the book advance for his client Stormy Daniels' and committing fraud in California. However, he does seem typical of the class of attorney who routinely attack the Trump family.

Had the Impeachment followed the model set forth by Nixon and Clinton, the DJIA could have fallen 42% on the sure-thing bet that caused Nixon to resign; it could have fallen 22% based on the reality Clinton had committed perjury and could have been declared guilty. But, at the beginning of November 2019, with impeachment looming, the DJIA had just broken through 27,000 and was heading back to the 15 July record high – by November 4th it had broken that record and continued to set new records with every hearsay witness and House spokesman assertion of "conclusive evidence."

All through the process, the DJIA was proclaiming the House case was nonsense. Then, after the New Hampshire primary and the Iowa Caucus debacle, on 12 February, it set a record high of 29,567 before drifting down in preparation for the quiet St Valentine's Day weekend that would only be marred by reports of new Coronavirus Disease 2019 (COVID-19) cases.

Back on 31 January, Alan Dershowitz had pointed out the weird logic put forth by Nadler and Schiff: *"If you have mixed motives, if you are in the public interest, and you're trying to help the public, but you're also trying to get re-elected, according to Schiff and Nadler, that's a crime."*

Thus, the House of Representatives took a position that, since any action seen as a positive on the campaign trail, if it involves the public interest or enforcing laws, it is a crime. Following their logic, all elected officials must avoid initiating actions until the are "lame ducks" and no longer seeking elective office. They cannot submit any legislation, nor have their name on it as a sponsor.

As Dershowitz phrased it:

"If you have any inkling of motive to help yourself get re-elected, they call that corrupt, and they say, even a tiny amount of motive to help yourself makes you into a criminal and makes you impeachable.

"And I turned to all the senators, and I said, everybody in this room, every senator, every politician everywhere always has one eye toward re-election, another eye toward the public interest. They almost always think it's the same. They also think their own election is in the public interest. You can't make that an impeachable offense."

The theory applies and could result in Joe Biden going to jail.

If Biden's motivation for getting Prosecutor General Shokin fired was the public interest and preventing corruption, but, in the back of his mind, he considered the benefits afforded his sin and the million dollars a year Hunter was making, Biden's subliminal motive was a personal benefit.

The very fact that Hunter was on the Board of Directors for Burisma Holdings, whose owner was being investigated and whose assets were being frozen by Shokin, according to Nadler and Schiff, that would be enough.

We can also look to the 2018 brag where we can see Biden say that Obama approved the cancellation of aid guarantees unless the Prosecutor General was fired. During the investigation, multiple House witnesses said or inferred Biden's actions were consistent with "Government Policy" and supported by the IMF and EU. If either Nadler or Schiff had been honest and competent in their investigation, they would have called Former President Obama to testify and verify that it was his policy – more important, they would have called him to testify, under oath, that he knew and approved of, the extortion or use of leverage bragged about by Biden.

However, we know that after Biden's brag, Obama declined to endorse him for President. Obama knows Biden; knows him to be unqualified for the Oval Office; knows that his extortion was not policy and certainly was not in American interests.

In the days and weeks following the acquittal, polls began to reveal the average voter was waking up, they were beginning to see the "Emperor's new clothes" were imaginary and a con. Then moved away from Biden, while Representative Eric Swalwell of California suggested the House should again walk the impeachment tightrope and, having failed, again seek to crash the financial markets. Then we have Speaker Pelosi, on 15 February, telling CNN's Christiane Amanpour, *"I can't even envision a situation where he would be re-elected."*

In Pelosi's view, anyone would be better than *"the current occupant of the White House."* This approach avoids endorsing any of the candidates, but it is also one that opens the door to a Billionaire racist responsible for an interesting bit of racial profiling: *"Ninety-five percent of your murders, murderers and murder victims, fit one M.O. You can just take the description, Xerox it, and pass it out to all the cops. They are male, minorities, 16 to 25. That's true in New York, that's true in virtually every city. And that's where the real crime is. You've got to get the guns out of the hands of people that are getting killed."*

That last sentence might be a misquote of the 2015 speech or it could have been a Freudian slip – but *"to get the guns out of the hands of people that are getting killed,"* sounds like Bloomberg was saying wanted the victims to be defenseless.

New York City is said to have the toughest gun control laws in the nation; the FBI figures for the nation – as of 2018 – had an estimated 16,214 people murdered, 44.6 percent were non-felony related arguments, and 39 percent were 'reasons unknown'. More important, access to guns or the race and ethnicity of those involved were not dominant factors.

In 2018 NYC had 289 murders, which prompted Mayor Bill de Blasio to say, *"We are the safest big city in America. But we always have more to do, and we will be doing more."* But, there is no way to properly evaluate the claim, other than being a combined effect of demographics and city layout. NYC has roughly 2-percent of the national population, but 60% of the murders per ten million people. In 2018, NYC accounted for roughly half of all murders in New York State; murder rates peaked during the federal level marked by the administrations of Nixon through Bush-41. As this also marked the period of tougher gun-restriction policies the "safety factor" seems unrelated to broader issues.

Using New York State as a focus for comparison, it appears that gun laws mean nothing in the overall context of crime and violence. The highest crime rates coincide with Baby-Boomers ages being between 5-25 in 1970; ending with them aged 25-45 in 1990. This also coincided with the nation promoting violence in Vietnam and then ending in with Bush-41 and Desert Storm. Apart from the Baby-Boomers being too old and there no longer being a Selective Service Draft, the high crime rates fell significantly into and after the 9/11 period – an overall timeframe when the median population age shifted from below twenty-eight to above thirty-three.

This infers that population age and Federal policies reflected in violence toward other nations are the controlling factors in crime and murder rates. This creates a strange paradox: at a time when the Federal policies are preparing an age group for killing others, it is necessary to increase police activities to prevent the violence from spilling over into and disrupting the domestic environment.

Psychologists have already linked age with crime; they might have already explored the idea that, since Brown and Black males are least likely to get college exemptions, they are most likely to begin early preparation for war zone survival by creating combat zones in their neighborhoods – gangs representing opposing armies.

Curiously, this could be a variation of Dershowitz, *"if you are in the public interest, and you're trying to help the public,"* where we see "survival" replace "public interest" in a context where victory in combat becomes the public interest objective – with a crime as an early model of preparation or training for destroying cultures *"in the public interest"* of regime change.

The verdict becomes *"in the public interest"* – necessitating a serious question of what that interest is. Should the House have the power to dictate to the Senate, and control whoever occupies the Oval? Is that *"in the public interest?"*

Concurrent with and after the verdict numerous campaign-related dynamics that kicked in and Progressive platforms were promoting things that both made absolute economic sense and were without the appropriate economic context.

While most voters ignore Biblical teachings, when we hear of free college, we should remember that the Biblical Merchant Tribe was pared with and required to support the Tribe of Scholars.

When hearing the platforms of Bernie Sanders or Elizabeth Warren, Evangelicals should immediately realize this era of America is striving toward the Biblical that they have always wanted. A Green New Deal is caring for the earth – true we have dominion over it, but we are also charged with its care and keeping. But that's a problem for any alleged evangelical who denies the human component in Global Warming – they had best pray there is no deity and no judgment day; Revelation 11:18 had best be a false prophecy because it promises to mark a time *"for destroying the destroyers of the earth."* (The Fossil Fuel Industry? Petroleum Nations?)

And how many times are readers of the Bible see: *"You shall not pollute the land in which you live, for blood pollutes the land..."* Does that mean pollution of the type we call pollution, and does it include the blood spilled in war?

America wastes more money on weapons of offensive blood spilling than the next twelve highest spending nations combined. Isn't it curious that trump minimizes offensive attacks and is yelled at for targeted drone strikes that achieve more in minutes that the Bush-43 war has in eighteen or nineteen years?

One aspect of the verdict has been the degree to which the public seems to love lies and hate Biblical or time-tested wisdom. In that regard, they focus on Trump's words, reshaping many of them to be saying what they want to hear rather than what was said. But, more important, ignoring the wisdom encapsulated in Matthew 7:

"15. Beware of the false prophets, who come to you in sheep's clothing, but inwardly are ravenous wolves.

"16. You will know them by their fruits. Grapes are not gathered from thorn bushes nor figs from thistles, are they?

"17. So every good tree bears good fruit, but the bad tree bears bad fruit.

"18. A good tree cannot produce bad fruit, nor can a bad tree produce good fruit.

"19. Every tree that does not bear good fruit is cut down and thrown into the fire.

"20. So then, you will know them by their fruits."

There's a beauty involved in the process. Invoke a verse from the Bible and even the Right-wing evangelicals will turn away when results {*"their fruits"*} matter more than words or deeds.

That's one of the beauties of informing people in a way they are sure not to heed, and therefore, they can be told but will not change their direction and so will not alter their fate.

What are the fruits and who are the false prophets?

The House Managers seem nice, but they lie and create webs of falsehoods based on supposition and unfounded hypotheticals – the result, an Impeachment without a crime and the argument that no crime is needed to Impeach. But they neglect to also assert that a crime is needed to convict. Instead, they yell about how pervasive and compulsive their "overwhelming evidence" was. But evidence of what? They provided no crime against which that evidence could be applied or tested.

On 12 January 2016, Science Daily reported that *"A team of researchers has found that overwhelming evidence without a dissenting opinion can in fact weaken the credibility of a case, or point to a failure of the system."*

We saw this affirmed by the House Managers or Adam Schiff and a nonexistent case against Trump. You were intended to accept the assumption Trump knew in June 2019 that Joe Biden would be the Democratic nominee – who would not be known until selected in a year later. You were also to believe that Barack Obama had approved extortion intended to fire a Ukrainian Prosecutor General and replace him with an engineer, rather than a lawyer – this was an engineer who had just been released from prison after serving time for fraud and corruption of the type the Prosecutor General Office was charged with investigating and prosecuting.

As pointed out in the article, the researchers cited *"an ancient Jewish law that said a suspect could not be convicted of a capital crime if all judges unanimously handed down a guilty verdict."* In terms of the House vote, the partisan nature of the decision points to the fact the decision is wrong. This was then proved when the House said they needed more evidence and testimony ordered by the Senate.

There was overwhelming testimony from people who did not see or hear anything. At the same time, they dismissed Biden's boast of using the full range of extortion, blackmail, and coercion to fire the Prosecutor General – and they claimed it was "Government Policy," which would mean Obama policy. A competent prosecutor would have called Obama to testify or provide a sworn deposition.

Extortion to force a change in foreign government official – where Biden boasted Obama would verify the threat – was an Obama order. Therefore Obama was the only witness who would eliminate any possibility of a Hunter Biden-Burisma motivation for the termination. Without that testimony, or worse, were Obama to deny that the extortion was on his orders, the critical aspect of the House argument goes out the window.

On the campaign trail, candidate Biden would then eliminate voter support by insulting voters. Still, when it came to asserting Trump could be beaten, Biden would assert running Mickey Mouse would see Mickey win.

Unfortunately, it's a mindless assertion, Donald Duck could also win – it would be a nice way to vote "none of the above." There is a problem. While fictional characters might make it onto the ballot and win the popular vote, they cannot be sworn in. They reflect a "pulse of the nation" vote – a protest vote. But why would people protest a strong economy, record economic expansion, low unemployment, and rising incomes?

The verdict shows the nation is split – almost cleanly — based on lies and unsupported assertion.

We know Warren is gullible enough to accept legend that she was sufficiently Native American to make it her racial identity. On 18 December 2019, she tweeted: *"Donald Trump has abused our diplomatic relationships and undermined our national security for his own personal, political gain. By voting to impeach him, the House has taken an important step to hold him accountable. I'm ready to fulfill my constitutional duty in the Senate."*

But, beyond the Adam Schiff fantasy, what evidence did she have? Her assertion infers she has evidence Biden had no personal motive for firing a lawyer who had frozen the assets of the firm paying his son and replacing him with an engineer. Is this the type of WMD start a 19-year war decision making American needs running the Oval Office?

Then there is Bernie Sanders, tweeting on the same day, *"The House of Representatives rightly carried out its constitutional responsibility by voting to impeach Donald Trump, the most corrupt president in our history. No one, including the president, is above the law."*

What are the specific actions Sanders is referring to?

In the world where we had Richard Nixon, or Bush-43 saying Bin Laden is irrelevant to the war on Terror, what renders Trump *"the most corrupt president in our history"*?

Is anything he has done exceed Watergate? Maybe it is worse than the bribery known as the *Teapot Dome scandal*? It would be nice to have something concrete to offset Biden's UkraineGate criminal conduct – or implicating Obama via a claim of approval.

Which Democratic nominee could complete the break and in so doing destroy the nation? Or will a Democratic descendant of the 4-Sisters emerge, replace Trump, and produce a secure Progressive nation?

The verdict yielded a result warned about in earlier volumes in this series – Trump seems to have made him stronger...improved his approval ratings.

He was acquitted along the same partisan lines that yielded the impeachment. The House took acted without logic or evidence of a crime; the Senate acquitted because there was no stated crime. The impeachment began on 9 November 2016, in December 2017 it was tabled; it was an attack in search of a justification, but served to distract from the emerging COVID-19 pandemic. The Swamp was fighting back against the man who said he would be draining it.

Lacking merit, the process was intended to harm the nation; worst of all, potential nominees were suckered into endorsing and then promoting it. As that realization sunk in among voters, Trump gained strength, but he was also distracted from the pandemic.

In December, Congressman Clay Higgins (R-LA) delivered an epic speech countering the rhetoric of Schiff and those who ranted about the need to expedite the impeachment. Higgins got biblical with his Conservative agenda talking points, so he declared: *"I have descended into the belly of the beast. I have witnessed the terror within. And I rise committed to oppose the insidious forces which threaten our Republic. America's being severely injured by this betrayal, by this unjust and weaponized impeachment, ... They are deep established D.C. They fear, they call this Republican map flyover country. They call us deplorables."*

Belonging to a repressive age that produced the Inquisitions and Salem Witch Trials, the talking points don't matter; they are not what defines America, but neither is impeachment used to distract from an emerging pandemic.

America is, and always has been, a nation of "*deplorables.*" It was revealed in JPC, where we tacked the American origins of all the practices we now associated with Nazi Germany. American bigots take interesting forms and shapes and often live in denial of their true nature.

During the 2020 SOTU address, the nation witnessed a broad showing of disrespect for 'Tuskegee Airmen" – the heroic African-American military bomber and fighter bomber pilots of World War Two – a few members of the small progressive Democrat conclave designated The Squad, declined their opportunity to salute Charles McGee.

Charles Edward McGee was born on December 7th, 1919 – He had just turned twenty-two when, describing the events that marked McGee's birthday, President Franklin Delano Roosevelt told a joint session of Congress that December 7, 1941, would be "*a date which will live in infamy.*" McGee joined the Air force and flew over 130 combat missions, and returned home to experience the racism that spawned the Civil Rights movement; he then served in Korea and Vietnam; upon reaching his century mark, receive an honorary rank of Brigadier General.

McGee, along with his great-grandson, Iain Lanphier, were being honored at the SOTU after the 100-year-old veteran of WWII, Korea, and Vietnam received an honorary rank of Brigadier General.

As part of his SOTU address, Trump cited the newly created United States Space Force and told the assembled legislature, "*Iain has always dreamed of going to space. He was the first in his class and among the youngest at an aviation academy. He aspires to go to the Air Force Academy, and then he has his eye on the Space Force. As Iain says, 'Most people look up at space. I want to look down on the world.'*"

Who knows, the USSF might become the non-fiction version of *Starfleet*, and Iain Lanphier the real-life incarnation of *Jonathan Archer*. What we do know is, exception for Ilhan Abdullahi Omar, Rashida Harbi Tlaib, and Mark William Pocan, when McGee and his great-grandson stood, an entire room of Republicans and Democrats gave a loud bipartisan standing ovation. A few days later, Pocan endorsed Bernie Sanders, and in doing so joined Tlaib and Omar who had done so before the Impeachment vote.

The verdict is in, the sides defined, the battle being waged.

CHAPTER NINE – Candidates

"We need to have a guaranteed healthcare coverage for everyone. The plan that I'm putting forward I call the Single Payer Plus Plan that's loosely modeled after Australia."

~ Rep. Tulsi Gabbard, THE HILL 27 December 2019

On 19 February, with the notable exception of Tulsi Gabbard, six candidates met at the Paris Theater in Las Vegas, Nevada and the primary target was a rather vulnerable former New York Mayor and Billionaire Mike Bloomberg – who bought his way onto the stage.

During the debate, the Fact-Checkers were having fun.

Using 2017 vs 2018 Census Bureau statistics, Bernie Sanders claimed Sanders' claim that "*the average American saw less than a 1 percent increase in their income.*"

While as accurate as any Lawyer's Lie, his use of "*Average*" as opposed to the Census Bureau "*Median*" distorts the reality of the inflation consistent growth rate against the Census Bureau numbers showing that median family incomes increased by 1.2 percent, while single household income increased by 2.4 percent. And even those numbers might be distorted by the prevailing demographics of the Baby-Boomer versus Baby-Buster income source disparity – couples going onto Social Security will see their incomes decrease, while the single person promoted to fill the retirement vacancy will likely see their income rise.

In all interpretations, since the Tax Cuts and Jobs Act of 2017 didn't take effect until 2018, any changes attributable to it are only going to show in the Census Bureau numbers.

In 2018, Real median household income was $63,179 versus $62,626 in 2017. We have more people entering the workforce, and that reduced the unemployment numbers. But, since many entered at the lower end of the employment pyramid, median household income posted (as of 20 February) for 2019 was $63,030 and lower than 2018. And the average individual income Sanders referred to cannot be determined without his source, but the average household income was $89,931 in 2019.

Assuming there is appropriate border control combined with the Wall achieving a decrease in undocumented immigrant traffic, and population demographics should push the economic expansion into 2024, while also creating a dramatic decrease in unemployment with unfilled jobs at the more skilled levels being filled by women currently in colleges across the nation.

Whoever was elected in November 2020 would inherit these demographics; if the open the Southern border, they destroy the growth that defines the economic reality that defines the economic recovery. If Obama's Fence become Trump's Wall and they remain in operation, the same demographics will allow for the introduction of M4A at a level that exceeds the Universal Healthcare currently in place throughout the rest of the industrialized world.

Addressing Climate Change issues Sanders said, *"This is an existential threat...this is a moral issue."* Warren assumed the basic approach of saying, *"I believe in science..."*

None of the candidates was about to deny a reality associated with Global Warming, but neither were they about to address the reality of Climate Refugees and the very real need to have systems in place to annually process the millions of people will overwhelm Mexican resources as they are forced north into regions of the United States where average daily temperatures are anticipated to exceed 120 degrees; therefore become functionally uninhabitable at the same time rising sea levels sink southern coast communities.

For all the nonsense of how a few individuals manage to scale the Wall, the reality remains its strongest purpose is crowd control. It remains with Congress, which had yet to legislatively address the 15 June 2012, Obama Executive Order entitled *Deferred Action for Childhood Arrivals (DACA)*, to create a modern Ellis Island – an area where Climate Refugees can be efficiently processed and set on a path to integration into the American culture.

Amy Klobuchar took on Buttigieg and called on Bloomberg to release his tax forms: *"Everyone up here has released their tax returns, mayor. And it is a major issue because the president of the United States has been hiding behind his tax returns, even when courts order him to come forward with those tax returns."*

Of course, three years in, Trump had yet to release personal tax documents. And, having failed to win any delegates, hedge-fund billionaire Tom Steyer was absent from the stage but, like all in the debate, he had done a disclosure in the form of about 3100 pages of meaningless documents.

With Klobuchar, there is the issue of her either supporting or opposing English as the official language of the nation. Bill Clinton had issued an executive order requiring federal agencies to provide documents in languages other than English, and in 2007 Klobuchar voted for its reversal. However, providing documents in a language newly-arrived individuals can understand does not diminish English as the primary or official language of the United States. However, that is something that will need to be formally addressed when the Climate Refugee issue ceases to be an elephant in the room and is no longer be ignored.

For now, the critical issue is Healthcare which, as the opening quote shows, Tulsi Gabbard is prepared to address in the manner Trump suggested it should be addressed – adapting and improving upon the Australian model. But, unless she makes the final round, her plan currently has no relevance.

Former Vice President Joe Biden has proposed expanding the Affordable Care Act by adopting auto-enrollment, offering a new public option for those in the individual market or having employer coverage, and he increases marketplace subsidies. There would also be some form of new long-term care tax credit and funding for rural health and mental health services would be increased.

The financing for the plan would involve raising taxes on high earner incomes, on capital gains and increasing taxes on heirs – via estate taxes. But the rich utilize foundations and trusts to bypass a range of taxes and the effect will be the traditional one where the promise is to tax the rich, but the poor and middle class take the hit.

Biden also believes he can enact reforms to lower healthcare costs and reduce prescription drug prices. But, so long as there is a private component, average people will pay more. However, as real as that might be, the propaganda focuses on the idea that people will "lose their private coverage" – they will lose "the plan they like" – so the fact that Universal Healthcare could provide superior coverage at a lower household cost doesn't enter into the discussion.

Pete Buttigieg proposes expanding the Affordable Care Act by increasing marketplace subsidies, expanding auto-enrollment, and offering a new "Medicare for All Who Want It" public option. There is also the idea of a retroactive enrollment process for those with an individual or employer-financed coverage. But again, the bowing to the private insurance industry increases costs through duplication of services and the cost of the private plans.

A proper universal health system would eliminate all out-of-pocket costs; this means no monthly premiums and no deductibles. It also means no employees paid to find excuses to deny coverage – as is the norm with private insurance companies. Universal health would mean, if you have a "Real ID" or a Healthcare card, you are covered and pay nothing.

How is it funded?

The funding is the same as for existing Medicare/Medicaid. All that is needed is a simple one-page legislative change eliminating the cap on Social Security payroll taxes. For millionaires, roughly six weeks into the year they reach the annual Payroll Tax Cap, which means their take-home pay increases by 6.3 percent of the gross – it also means their employer is also richer in terms of the matching payments obligation. As a result, Social Security tax "burdens" fall more heavily on those who make less. And, due to poor health care and other factors, those who make less are likely to die younger.

Social Security functions as originally designed – a tax that low-income people will willingly pay because it promises them the future benefit they are unlikely to collect. Those earning the median household income represent half the households; median individual income in 2019 was $40,100 and the average individual income was $58,379.45. We can play with numbers and the threshold for the 1% cited in debates and on the campaign trail is $328,551.

When we say Median income we are talking about an equal number above and below that point; Average income is the total of all incomes divided by all the earners contributing to that total. The goal should be to get the Median equal to or above the Average. And that does not mean making people poorer, rather it means making all Americans richer – ideally in a global economy where our richest are richer than the rich in other nations. Phrased another way, the average American worker should be comfortably in the global 1% of Industrialized Nations.

In terms of funding Universal Healthcare, it would be wise to remove the Payroll Tax Cap; immediately raise the Minimum Wage to levels that remove all workers from SNAP or welfare subsidies.

The increased Payroll Tax revenues, combined with the cost savings for the payroll subsidies, would more than pay for Health care for every citizen. Private and employer insurance would be needed for those who are not yet full citizens.

The Payroll Cap limits payments to the first $137,700; thus, someone making $1,000,000 per year is paid-in-full on 19 February; everyone in the 1% is fully paid by the end of 28 May. That means, for seven months out of the year, there is less monthly revenue for Medicare and Social Security, than was received in the first three months of the year. Since the benefits are paid for all twelve months, it follows that there would be diminishing revenues and reserves as inflation or market forces carry more workers over that magic $137,700 mark.

It was a time-bomb created and installed under Reaganomics where debt would be monetized through inflation and all benefits not hardwired to real inflation would lose their purchasing power. It was all "voodoo economics" and it didn't matter because it would explode when the Baby-Boomers were ready to collect – which was three or more decades after the economic bomb was planted.

In a tweet dated 21 February, investigative journalist Jeremy Scahill wrote:

"I have what is considered to be excellent health insurance. My family spent approximately $15,000 out of pocket in 2019. I do not love my 'excellent,' employer-based health insurance. In fact, it's awful."

An income search showed Scahill earned roughly twice the payroll maximum and placing him comfortably among the 1% which constitutes the modern economic whipping boy.

If the payroll cap was removed, Scahill could receive better medical care through a M4A structure than he does on his policy – and he would save money. Understand what that means in terms of real disposable income – provide M4A, is funded by lifting the wage payroll cap, and the 99% gain disposable cash. If you also consider that VA medical coverage or other government-funded medical care (including Medicaid) would all be provided by M4A and there are "savings' created by government elimination of related duplicated bureaucratic infrastructure and paperwork.

In terms of the ACA cost structure, there is no rational reason for citizens to pay "for insurance" when it's already covered by the withholding taken from their salary. And we need to focus on dual structures – one for citizens and then everyone else. A non-citizen or households with non-citizen residents might be subject to some form of a surcharge. Alternatively, non-citizens might fall into the group that receives employer or private insurance until they become citizens.

The Scahill example shows him paying a quarter of what the average individual earns. That means eliminating the threat of that cost, or the real cost of needing but not having medical coverage, it becomes clear that the average individual can contribute to the GDP and economic growth of the nation by not having to worry about any medical expenses.

Bernie Sanders proposed lifting the payroll cap to $250,000 or more – but that does not automatically adjust for inflation, while completely removing the came adjusts as the money is earned. He has also suggested expanding Social Security *"benefits across-the-board, including a $1,300 a year benefit increase for seniors with incomes of $16,000 a year or less."*

Part of the "problem" or a real issue for voters is the changes in income in terms of daily reality. Many candidates have addressed the issue of student loan debt. Higher education is more important in 2020 than it has ever been in the national history. If we look back to an immigration era-defining seventy years ending in 1950, a High School Diploma was rare and people would speak of "the first person in the family to graduate college."

One point, the major costs of a family were housing, health care, and transportation, now education has been added and 2018 was compared to 1985 to see how things have changed.

In 1985, all four costs could be covered with 30 weeks of work – by 2018, that number had grown to 53 weeks and explains the growth in education-related debt. The author of the comparative study, Oren Cass of the Manhattan Institute for Policy Research, stated: *"By conventional measures, material living standards everywhere in the income distribution are at all-time highs, and technological progress continues to improve them. Yet many jobs able to support a family in the past no longer do."*

Product improvements which are counted in improved living standard are not relevant to meeting the cost of the four basics – if anything, changes in the standard of living mask the reality that is the actual act of living and progressing up the economic ladder. The standard measure of income increase progression against inflation fails because it looks at a standard "shopping cart" and not the real costs of life preparation as represented by education. There was a time when people could say the "worked their way through college" and when the graduated they had a debt-free diploma. No Longer!

A high school student cannot get a part-time or full-time job which will cover tuition and basic living expenses. After World War Two we had the GI Bill. At the time it a benefit to grow the economy and reward veterans many of whom were married and certainly they were older than the traditional college freshman. After 9/11 there was another GI Bill, but that doesn't help the average American.

When we look at Bernie Sanders we see a man with a valid message who is the wrong messenger for the United States. He is not a POTUS Cousin and not a descendant of the 4-Sisters. But he was defining the early caucus and primary states; more important, he represented the Jewish Grandfather everyone loves and so his base became the 17-29-year-olds who longed for that connection to the past. As a Democratic-Socialist Sanders offers them a traditional Progressive movement dating back to 1848 when it gave additional energy to the anti-slavery movement in the United States and was a driving force behind the Social Security movement in Germany.

Sanders is one of the last of "Silent Generation"; the average "Millennial" is the grandchild of "Baby-Boomers"– those who were in their first eight formative years when McCarthyism dominated television, which was the epitome of modern communications at the time and children were as enraptured by those screens in the same way they are now enamored of internet-linked devices. During the madness that was the bigotry and antisemitism of McCarthyism, the terms Socialism and Communism became synonymous within the popular vernacular and ingrained in the minds of Baby-Boomers.

Those born between 1946 and 1964 are dealing with minds conditioned by McCarthyism, the Korean War, and Vietnam. It will be hard for them to shake the indoctrination they received during the first eight years of their lives. And, in 2020 and 2024, they are going to have a hard time relating to function with a minimum wage structure that is designed to keep full-time workers on welfare.

To mitigate the growing economic threat, the United States will need a Minimum wage that is fixed at 175% of the poverty rate – based on a 35-hour work-week. This would remove all full-time workers from the welfare subsidy roles. It would also be wise to tax 'unearned income' over $1,000 – including interest, dividends, and capital gains – with a flat tax of 6.5% that is deductible from total income, and serves as an equivalent to workers portion of the payroll tax.

Then there is Minimum Retirement Social Security.

Any citizen with ten years social security covered work history is entitled to a minimum benefit equal to 150% of poverty. Benefit levels should be scaled up from there to around 450% of poverty as a maximum benefit. Disability benefits and those for legal residents can be different, and, in two worker families, both should be entitled to collect their full earned benefits.

The demographics are important and will remain so through 2050 when the vast majority of Baby-Boomers will have died. And Generation-X could push that to 2060. In both cases, it is likely the number of citizen workers will be less than beneficiaries – Climate Refugees will serve to increase the number of workers, but they are likely to be on the lowest economic tier and therefore coontributing the least amount to what has been a pay-as-you-go system.

Candidate Sanders has been promoting the publicly-funded "Medicare for All" (M4A) program that would provide health and long-term care benefits for all U.S. residents – properly, this should be all citizens, not residents. The difference is small but significant in terms of Climate Refugees who are documented non-citizens. All others can have some form of Obamacare or private coverage paid for as individuals or through their employer.

The last thing the nation needs to is to create incentives for the sick or disabled to migrate to the United States – let them pass on to Canada to increase Canada's California size population.

Naturally, Sanders would impose the type of price controls a contract plan would normally have for provider payments, and drug prices would be consistent with an international index. As we have seen, unlike the stated Sanders plan to increases in tax rates for workers and employers as well as a series of targeted tax increases focused on higher earners, wealthy households, and businesses, the existing payroll tax system could be easily be modified in a way that effectively expands it to include a vast untapped income base.

Senator Elizabeth Warren has also proposed a "Medicare for All" program that would provide health and long-term care benefits to all U.S. residents with virtually no out-of-pocket costs or provider networks; there would also be several targeted spending increases; payments would at comparable to Medicare rates, and have targeted reforms to reduce provider payments. Under her plan, prescription drug prices would be negotiated and brought into line with those in other nations. Again, the proposed changes in the existing payroll tax structure would probably be superior to Warren's anti-wealth tax structure.

Warren suggested immigration reform and defense cuts as an additional source of funding. But immigration reform requires an understanding and full acceptance of Climate Change reality – that Climate Refugees will be created internally and externally as a result geographical regions experience normal temperatures exceeding 120 degrees Fahrenheit.

America needs to decide if the idea of Universal healthcare is a Leftist or Centrist concept – or is it a basic human necessity that should transcend Party or political lines?

We know the mandate embodied in the Biblical parable of the Good Samaritan – the gift of medical care goes further and extends to also providing recovery care. And, in the parable, we are told a bit of the victim's back-story, but the Samaritan knows nothing of it. All he knows is there is an injured person in need of help. The Samaritan exits without any thought or action that would infer they sought repayment.

The parable creates a pragmatic problem. The religious or moral thing is to assist those in need – but it should not be done to the exclusion of those providing the care. That is why there should be a three-tier system: M4A for citizens, ACA for legal Residents, and a state or local level program for the undocumented whose bodies serve to bolster the Representational population count. Sanctuary districts should not be able to bleed Federal government programs of resources that taxpayers provide their fellow citizens.

We should ask how the Right-wing justifies calling abortion murder – the Bible provides for abortion if a fetus does not belong to the husband. But if they want to insist upon outlawing abortion, then they cannot, rationally or morally, refuse to provide necessary pregnancy and postpartum medical care. And in the case of a fetus known to be non-viable, they are not discussing a potential person who will grow to contribute to society and fulfill their proper role in the culture. So why do they insist on inflicting pain and suffering on their fellow citizens and compound it with the cost and potential death of the mother? Is it that, to use their terminology, they are in truth worshipers and servants of Satan?

When a candidate makes a public showing of their attendance at a religious service, they reveal their pandering to religion.

It's an old debate taking on an interesting twist: Senator Bernie Sanders, a democratic socialist, has a solid base that carried forward from the 2016 nomination process. He's an Independent running on the Democratic ticket and doesn't represent the party or its voter base. In Iowa and New Hampshire, traditional Democratic moderates – Senator Amy Klobuchar and Mayor Pete Buttigieg – had more votes than Sanders.

Keeping with the POTUS COUSIN and 5-Sister tradition that defined the first 57 quadrennial era, and has begun the second cycle, a Bernie Sanders nominee could win in 2020, but would likely not be inaugurated – his POTUS Cousin Vice President would become POTUS-46.

We could Sanders team-up with Mike Buttigieg or Elizabeth Warren and win the 2020 election, but to properly feel the burn, Bernie Sanders would need to take the second slot.

Buttigieg and Warren are the POTUS Cousins; Klobuchar and Sanders are outside the family and American tradition. Looking at the former Vice President, Joe Biden, we have the obvious problem of a braggart who thought it humorous that he successfully extorted Ukraine into firing a Prosecutor General – possibly using his office for the private or personal economic benefit of his family – and his senility was such that he bragged of it in front of C-SPAN cameras.

Tulsi Gabbard is a solid POTUS Cousin and descendant of the 4-Sisters who has shown she doesn't quit. The process sidelined her but, "*Nevertheless, she persisted.*"

While the candidates were forming a circular firing squad, it was Gabbard was speaking to the voters and saying:

"As president I'll protect social security by (#1) ensuring no one "raids" the social security fund to pay for other things within government, and (#2) eliminate the cap so the wealthiest Americans pay their fair share into social security."

While Gabbard was talking about economics, which Sanders had touched on early in the campaign be had since abandoned, he was on the campaign trail promoting variations on House Manager post-impeachment talking points: "*We are going to defeat Donald Trump because the American people know that he is running a corrupt administration... that not only is he a liar, he is a fraud.*"

Granted, long ago, Donald John Trump has adopted his PT Barnum persona and it helped him achieve media success with *The Celebrity Apprentice*, and he is being attacked to continuing his catchphrase *"You're Fired"* as a mode to control the strengthening of the American economy to maintain the longest economic expansion in the nation's history. We could say *"the Deep State"* has expressed its anger at having the Swamp Drained and the exposed denizens removed.

In the Johnson-Carter eras, outsourcing had resulted in a reality where, when Reagan took office, Germany's Volkswagen was the only car company making cars in America. Concurrent with the Impeachment vote, Trump mentioned,*"Ford Motor Company just announced that it is investing $1.5 billion in two auto factories in the Detroit area, creating another 3,000 Michigan jobs."*

At the same time, Tulsi Gabbard was tweeting:

"We must not continue wasting trillions on regime change wars, the new Cold War & nuclear arms race. Our precious resources must be used for the needs of the American ppl. It's time to stand up for quality affordable healthcare, education, environmental protection & more. Join me."

Major Gabbard recognizes and addresses two complementary realities. First, it is necessary to reverse and negate a Reaganomics style economic tradition whose policies were predicated on an over-application of Laffer Curve observations which described the British tax policies that discouraged investment.

The tax revenue maximization curve devised by Arthur Laffer in 1967 identified a point where taxes made the potential profit on investment simply not worth the potential loss from that same investment. The curve is asymmetrical and does not conform to Bell Curve analytics and so places the peak tax rate at about 70% before the before trigger revenue losses. Arguably, a long-term violation of the curve would damage the long-term strength of the national economy.

The second element of Gabbard's focus evaluates where the nation is and then projecting where it should strive to be. This is an aspect of a "soak-the-rich" tax approach seen in a Warren or Sanders approach. Accumulation of wealth is something to be encouraged. As mentioned above, we need to lift the poor.

Under Reagan, we heard the empty slogan about "a rising tide lifts all boats" and then saw the focus become dumping water into the holds of the largest ships so they could sail off and leave small boat beached. To raise the economic waters, you need to raise the minimum wage and eliminate as many basic expenses as possible – for all people. Don't yell just became the wealthy also gain the same free healthcare benefit or some other benefit which lifts the poor out of poverty.

In keeping with Socialist-Marxist base terminology, the idea is to share the *surplus capital* The basic economic theory did not rely on stealing capital from the wealthy, it was to allow everyone to meet their basic needs and have disposable income. To do that, the State would use its revenues to meet common needs – police, roads, bridges, basic housing, medical care, old-age income, and anything else which allows a base level of human dignity.

Another underlying premise or assumption is wealth might not last. We demonize those who can pass their wealth or the skills that allowed the wealth accumulation, to their children. In the case of Donald Trump, he inherited his grandfather's knowledge as filtered through his father. But we all want to bestow an inheritance on our children – read the Bible, there are thirteen tribes but only twelve had an "inheritance" in the land or a defined territory; the thirteenth was the Levite/Kohanim who ruled; in America, we can talk of the descendants of the 5-Sister as our Levites. In the Bible, the worthy "marry-up", they will marry into the Levites within their tribe and then their children can marry across the tribal boundaries.

In America, we need to provide the basics and thus allow the worthy among the lowest to join the highest. We cannot have, we must refrain from having, a society be like that of ancient India and have a class of "untouchables" – that's what happens when you force people to be dependant upon SNAP and other subsidies even when they work full-time, or have worked and, now in old age, find their benefits for a lifetime of contributing to or investing in the economy has made them poor because some president did something that triggered a recession from which they could not recover.

In terms of the candidates, we could look back to comments by Barack Obama that can easily be interpreted to reflect a rejection of Sanders, Biden, and Bloomberg:

"Women 'indisputably better' as leaders, 'old men' get in the way."

As reported on the BBC, Obama said at a Singapore event:

"Now women, I just want you to know; you are not perfect, but what I can say pretty indisputably is that you're better than us [men].

"I'm absolutely confident that for two years if every nation on earth was run by women, you would see a significant improvement across the board on just about everything... living standards and outcomes.

"If you look at the world and look at the problems, it's usually old people, usually old men, not getting out of the way.

"It is important for political leaders to try and remind themselves that you are there to do a job, but you are not there for life, you are not there in order to prop up your own sense of self-importance or your own power."

It appears Obama finds fault with those *"Silent Generation"* candidates; nor is he enamored with early Baby-Boomers – but he does man an exception for women. But then, Obama is twenty years younger than the three oldest male candidates, who were all born around the same time or earlier than his mother. In many ways, his words could describe his attitude toward his mother, whose death was at the age he was soon after beginning his second term – *"that you are there to do a job, but you are not there for life."*

During the Nevada debate, Warren said: *"We're Democrats, we don't take away healthcare. Republicans do."* But that's only because Republicans are hooked on the private sector, and the private sector is not what you want for healthcare or a failed private prison system which my daughter Beryl CD Lipton, an investigative reporter with the FOIA group MuckRock has studied and reported on for years. Bernie Sanders opposes privatized prisons, as should any rational candidate.

No nation on earth has universal healthcare, certainly, none has care like that which could be delivered via M4A – with higher care and less cost, if done properly. In Austria, the marginal tax rate is 40% on incomes over 35,000%, on top of a regressive value-added tax. In Finland, a 57% marginal tax rate applies to income above 37,000 euros, again, ignoring the VAT. These are examples of the middle class paying far more for healthcare system with wait times Americans would never tolerate.

America can do better, and should, after the election.

STEP ASIDE FOR IMPEACHMENT SURROGATE

As we settle into this point in of this book, Super Tuesday is exactly one week away and external natural forces are impacting the economy. On 12 February, the DJIA close peaked at 29,551.42 when the Coronavirus Disease 2019 (COVID-19) seemed to be controlled. But then it appeared outside of China and the DJIA turned down.

On 21 February, the DJIA entered the weekend at 28,992.41 and opened on Monday, 24 February, at 28,402.93, finishing the day at 27,960.80 – booking a loss of 3.56%, having fallen 1,031.61 points, and Tuesday saw a drop of 879.44 (3.15%). A support level was marked on the 28th and on 2 March a rebound of 1,293.96 was seen as prelude to a Super Tuesday 'give-back'.

The first pneumonia cluster was identified in Hubei Province China on New Year's Eve; on 7 January it was confirmed COVID-19 was novel. At the time, House Speaker Nancy Pelosi was holding the Articles of Impeachment – had they contained a legitimate or any defined crime, based on the Clinton Impeachment, the DJIA would have fallen at least 25%; if the crime were serious, following the Nixon model, the fall was 45% before his resignation.

On 27 February, Warren submitted a one page fund transfer bill that would stop work on the southern border to fund COVID-19 treatments; within days there were five confirmed virus cases in Mexico – so among population who would welcome an open border.

Saudi Arabia closed its borders to religious pilgrims visiting Muslim Holy Sites – had Trump done it would be a "racist action" not warranted by health and safety considerations – but it echoes a China flight ban Trump imposed in January, when there were only 12,000 confirmed infections in China. Warren's open border action coincided with 83,365 infections reported globally, 78,824 in China. But Warren was endangering border communities and California.

As the cases crew, Trump was being attacked for not taking action fast enough yet, there were less than 3,554 cases when Trump announced his intention to impose a travel ban – the timing gave an early warning to airlines- and it was initiated before the known cases reached 9,692.

On 28 February, the DJIA closed at 25,409.36 after making a low of 24,681.01. The DJIA high was 29,568.57 on 12 February – which says the Market analysts weren't concerned as early as the President was. So Trump was ahead of the market analysts.

CHAPTER TEN – **Pandemic**

"The great enemy of the truth is very often not the lie, deliberate, contrived and dishonest, but the myth, persistent, persuasive and unrealistic."

~John F. Kennedy

At this point in our ongoing historical record, COVID-19 has imposed itself as a disruptive replacement or surrogate for the Never Trump impeachment movement. Their goal was to stop the record economic expansion and, ideally, crash the economy. So long as *"it is the economy stupid"* is the primary voter motivation, necessarily, those who want to make Russia happy will devote themselves to the task of undermining confidence in Trump.

When discussing the economy, it is necessary to discuss the financial markets and, as measured by the DJIA, over 16-days, the low was 16.5% below the high; in terms of the chartist approach, it had reached or tested its support level on 28 February.

At the beginning of 2019, the media reported on Chinese pork imports being infected with African Swine Fever; this overlapped the US-China agricultural trade war; initially, Chinese officials declared it would have no impact on pork availability. Pork constitutes an unhealthy dietary mainstay of the Chinese diet – as pointed out in a Communist Party newspaper article entitled *"It is Better to Eat Less Pork."*

Health official Xu Shufang was cited in the article as saying, *"Actually, no matter whether pork is expensive or not, everybody should improve their diet to eat a little less pork and a little more white meat."*

She and colleague both pointed out that pork has the effect of promoting obesity; it has been long known that pork fat also clogs arteries, promoting heart attacks or circulatory problems; the saturated fat increases harmful LDL cholesterol, impedes flow in smaller blood vessels and can kill brain cells, diminishing brain capacity – Silent Generation and Baby-Boomers recall the running joke in the Li'l Abner that equated his pork chop diet with his lack of intellect, a secondary effect not associated with China.

The forced culling of millions of infected pigs helped ease the trade war tensions. Given a billion-plus Chinese consumer demand for both pork and the soy needed for pig-feed, American agricultural health standards placed its farm products ahead of the competition.

The 2016 election bolstered the myth and legend of Donald John Trump and the impeachment without a crime that was based on a POTUS investigating a former Vice President who publically gave a bragging rendition of an illegal act committed while in office. The described criminal extortion was pre-approved and authorized by President Obama.

The coastal elites were threatened by Trump's elimination of the Swamp Denizens, and used the quietly conducted investigation to justify impeachment; by so doing, they made Biden's crime public and dismissed as "Government Policy." In February 2020, Ukraine prosecutors responded to a criminal complaint filed by the Shokin – something which might not have happened if California Swamp Denizens had not gone public with Biden's act of extortion.

The coastal elites defined the swamp that needed draining – to some they were foolish people who have mismanaged the country for their own greedy purposes, acting in that capacity they defended Joe Biden, who publically detailed his criminal actions at a forum being documented by C-SPAN. Then, compounding the dishonesty, the coastal elites declared that Trump was motivated by something he described as "horrible" but rather was motivated by some fear of Biden – the pre-ordained Democratic nominee – and therefore the President's re-election rival President who could only be defeated if a foreign government provided politically useful "dirt" on him.

Successful Presidents are mythmakers whose story details the defeat overwhelming opposition while providing some meaning to events that define their era while shaping the future definition of true heroes and dastardly villains. Once the challenge or threat is accepted as central to the myth, that same myth explains why the individual arose as the perfect predestined anti-hero who would save the day and therefore the kingdom, nation, or culture.

The times suit the mythology that will mark quadrennial 59 and prepare the United States for mystical 60 which will bring the nation the Progressive Era Theodore Roosevelt promoted during his two terms and then later he created the Bull Moose Party – a period that spanned quadrennial 28-30 (1901-1912) and saw the American Medical Association oppose the idea of Universal Health care.

The life and times of Teddy Roosevelt have a mythical aura.

But, his era was not the "right time" in American history – which proved to be the second 19 quadrennial or quadrennial 38 (1941) and the entry of the United States into World War Two – under President Franklin Delano Roosevelt (FDR), who proved to be the right Roosevelt at the right time, and became the only person elected to four consecutive terms as President.

In many ways, the Roosevelt line determined our values and changed the face of our society. But it also opened that gate or path to a world-view the made America the global policemen and a force for imposed regime change that had resulted in an economy busting military-budget.

If Bernie Sanders was "of the ancient mythical line," he would offer something to augment the mythology of the era. Myths tend to have primary and secondary heroes outside conventional images – Robin Hood, an outlaw opposed by Sheriff of Nottingham, is the hero and the symbol of law is a villain; in the era of Trump, Adam Schiff is Nottingham, a liar prosecutor, who inventing any reason the swamp denizens can use to justify bringing down the wicked liar of Sherwood Forest (or Mar-A-Largo).

There is always a Maid Marian, a Friar Tuck, Little John, Will Scarlet, and any number of supporting characters we can selectively identify with as those who are always somewhere among the heroes and antiheroes of life and myth.

In a mythical age, at the beginning of a new cycle in history, where would a Bernie Sanders fit in? Or an Elizabeth Warren? And then we have Tulsi Gabbard – is she the true hero? Will she be the one who changes things? If not in 2020, then in 2024, a year when the mystical numbers are positioned to agree with historic events.

Maybe Warren is the Trump era Maid Marion – a ballad says when they first met she fought:

They drew out their swords, and to cutting they went,

At least an hour or more,

That the blood ran apace from bold Robins face,

And Marian was wounded sore.

What modern myth has America constructed to define both the Trump-era, and how do Sanders, Warren, Biden, and Bloomberg fit into it?

Joseph R Biden is no Robin Hood confronting Covid-19.

When looking at those who would lead the nation in 2021, we see none who will be there in 2025. In 2025, who will conform to the JFK observation:

"Mothers all want their sons to grow up to be president, but they don't want them to become politicians in the process."

Does the United States need a leader who conforms perfectly to the role of the professional politician? Is that the character of one who is the ideal or desired protagonist of our new mythology?

At the CNN Town Hall on 20 February, Elizabeth Warren stated the reality of immigration and what should be the goal after Trump's Wall is completed and there are official crossing points in place where Climate Refugees can be processed: "*Immigration does not make this nation weaker – immigration makes this country stronger. We need to expand legal immigration, and that means a pathway to citizenship for all of our neighbors, friends, and loved ones who are here.*"

Having a pathway to citizenship is one thing, but two months earlier Bernie Sanders had Tweeted: *"If working people—the vast majority of our country—don't have income to spend on goods and services, we can't create jobs.   There is a limit to how many limousines and yachts you can have. When so few have so much, it is not only a moral issue, it is also an economic issue."*

Accepting immigrants requires the ability to afford them, the nation needs to have workers – ideally, those immigrants will enter with the skills the nation needs and which will support the workers as they move toward being full citizens. During the first 300-years of American history, this was not a problem.

The nation then went through the transition period known as the twentieth-century, and everything changed. With the dawn of the twenty-first century, the era of education and high-technology came into existence; working the land, being a peddler, a tailor, a shoemaker, and all those other necessary jobs which could be done with a minimal education was no longer acceptable.

Times have changed.

Covid-19 underscored the degree of change. Over a four to five year period – between 1347 and 1352 – a pandemic called the Black Plague devastated Europe, killing an estimated 25-30 million people. In the era of Bubonic plague, no airplanes existed to carry the infected across continents and ships were slow.

Flea invested rats would board the ships; infected fleas would infect the crew, who would die before reaching a distant port. Those who were coastal traders might spread the plaque locally, otherwise, they might fall ill and be identified as a plague ship. A lack of proper hygiene and crude medical knowledge kept the pandemic local.

In the modern world, the fleas have become people.

In the modern world, medical knowledge is not the primary issue. That issue is funding – money. And on 24 February, Trump requested $2.5 Billion to meet Covid-19 response issues; Speaker Nancy Pelosi responded by saying, "*The House will swiftly advance a strong, strategic funding package that fully addresses the scale and seriousness of this public health crisis.*"

Soon after that, Senate Minority Leader Chuck Schumer was ranting about the request being "inadequate", and proposed $8.5 Billion. At 9:02 AM on 25 February President Trump reacted, via Twitter, saying: "*Cryin' Chuck Schumer is complaining, for publicity purposes only, that I should be asking for more money than $2.5 Billion to prepare for Coronavirus. If I asked for more he would say it is too much. He didn't like my early travel closings. I was right. He is incompetent!*"

Twenty-four hours later Republicans and Democrats were in meetings behind closed doors negotiating an emergency funding bill of between $6 billion and $8 billion; seven days later, on 4 March, it was announced that the agreement would be for $7.8 billion in new appropriations, with an additional $500 million to replenish the account drained by the initial response; then, on the 6th Trump signed the final $8.3 billion package.

On Super Tuesday, a tornado struck Nashville, Tennessee and resulted in 25 dead with an additional 38 missing and unaccounted for – an overnight event killing twice, possibly six times, the virus deaths since first reported domestic case a month earlier.

Super Tuesday also saw JAMA (Journal of American Medical Association) run an article entitled "*Wasteful Health Care Spending in the United States*" in which it was stated that previous "*estimates of wasteful spending to between $760 billion and $935 billion per year, or approximately 25% of total US health care expenditures*" had been updated to reflect the fact that the waste reflects defects in care delivery related to suboptimal clinical decisions perpetuated by a system of misaligned incentives. The co-payments for necessary care, combined with incentives for clinicians to provide episodic rather than coordinated care, plus additional incentives for health systems to react to acute illness rather than coordinate care prevent acute illness.

The updated analysis did not alter the amount of waste, rather it identified 10 modifiable risk factors where waste could be attributed and equal "*22% of all health care expenditures – $750 billion each year.*"

In the context of Covid-19, the United States has created incentives for individuals to avoid early treatment of symptoms and that means avoiding early detection of future diseases – ones that prove to be true pandemic and far more deadly than the current one targeting the elderly or medically frail.

On 7 October 2019, the JAMA article being updated pointed out: "*The United States spends more on health care than any other country, with costs approaching 18% of the gross domestic product (GDP). Prior studies estimated that approximately 30% of health care spending may be considered waste.*" This was then followed by a breakdown of annually wasted funds by area, and it was stated: "*administrative complexity, $265.6 billion.*" This infers the simple act of consolidating Medicare/Medicaid and VA under a common single-payer system that is then expanded to Medicaid for All (M4A) would, over ten years, save $2.6 trillion.

If other savings – including preventative care prior to acute illness onset – were implemented, there is the possibility of a $9 trillion saving. In context, in February 2020 the National Debt was $23.25 trillion. By eliminating the Payroll Tax contribution cap and adding a fractional percentage to cover preventative health care, the savings would quickly erase those portions of the National Debt which are not directly related to Social Security obligations or the various forms of domestic savings associated with Treasury Bonds.

Of course, in the context of any pandemic, there is a practice common in the United State to want to encourage the worst possible outcome and so it follows that in Maine, Super Tuesday also saw a referendum vote on whether or not to retain a new law that bans non-medical exemptions for vaccines required for children to attend school in the state.

The intent of the law, LD 798, which came into effect in May 2019, was to ban the use of religious and philosophical objections as a basis to opt-out of vaccines for school-aged children. Maine voters overwhelming agreed the law should remain on the books. Had they decided it should be repealed, parents could reject flu vaccinations for their children, thereby increasing the likelihood of a pandemic like that in 1918 or, when we have a vaccination for COVID-19, its reemergence and spread in 2021.

One interesting discovery or observation with COVID-19 in China has been the extent to which it seems to have little effect on children. With 81,008 people contracting the virus, and 3,255 have died, children appear to contract only mild forms of the disease. Only about 2.4% of cases have been children. As stated by Dr. Frank Esper, a pediatric infectious diseases specialist at Cleveland Clinic Children's Hospital, "*Normal coronaviruses seem to affect children and adults equally, but this one, for whatever reason, certainly skews more to the adult population.*"

The fact that children are less symptomatic does not remove the reality that they can be carriers.

Another observation is the infection rate where air quality is poor or among smokers; the common element is lung damage that weakens the immune system, but which might be addressed as the population moves away from fissile fuels.

Vaccines work. Edward Jenner introduced the first Smallpox Vaccine in 1796 and 200-years later it had been declared effectively eradicated from the planet. Modern vaccines don't require such an extended time span in which to do their job – assuming people want the disease to be eradicated.

We've alluded to anti-vaxxer mentality as part of that group whose approach always seeks the most harm to the most people – thus they oppose Obamacare and promote open borders. We are in the age of people wanting to disrupt society; we saw it with the insistence upon an impeachment without a crime as a response to the Constitution functioning properly. We can, in terms of POTUS COUSINS and descendants of the 4-Sisters, assert it even served to maintain historic continuity.

The withdrawals prior and after Super Tuesday also showed the same continuity process in which only the candidate who has a history of promoting solid universal health care remained in the running. Bernie Sanders does not meet the subliminally defined and imposed historically consistent ancestral criteria.

Billionaires Mike Bloomberg and Tom Steyer did not fit the criteria and demonstrated that even vast wealth cannot overcome a historic subliminal criterion – as a result, they were eliminated by the nomination process. As was made evident in the previous book in this series, Elizabeth Warren was also eliminated – she couldn't even carry her own state.

The process showed it worked to eliminate the non-POTUS COUSINS; it also narrowed the field in terms of a Gerontocracy that accompanied the last hurrah for the Silent and Boomer generations. Warren was the youngest of the Gerontocracy generation was the basis of the final two quadrennial cycles of the first full era of United States history.

Trump represents the early Baby-Boomers, while Sanders or Biden will represent the last of Silent Generation; moving forward, the election choices existed in the context of a threatened pandemic that holds children relatively immune while targeting the infirm or Gerontocracy.

Gerontocracy, or *"government based on rule by old people,"* has had its place in history. It is the ancient concept of "wisdom of the elders" – but that concept emerged in ancient times when only the wise or genetically gifted survived. The ability to survive was the definitive definition of leadership or worthiness warranting listening to.

If we look at Otto von Bismarck and his 1883 introduction of Social Security, we see a gift for the elderly that was a disguised tax on the average person – which they happily paid as a bet they would beat the odds and live the twenty-extra-years beyond the average life expectancy. The age of 65 was selected because most people never came close to reaching it and therefore would never collect on the tax they happily paid. Those who lived to collect had clearly done something in their life that gave them an advantage over everyone else in their generation – and that knowledge was desirable.

The 1883 date was the beginning of the process, it marked the introduction of a compulsory sickness insurance law in Germany – in today's political environment, the rest of the Industrialized World has adopted state-provided healthcare. In 1912, President Theodore Roosevelt became an advocate and the platform of Bernie Sanders shows that America has yet to get a message often spoken of in terms of the Biblical Good Samaritan. National health care should be a priority in a nation as economically advanced as the United States.

Interestingly, a newspaper report on 11 January 1983 stated: *"Biden suggested a gradual increase in the retirement age would help improve the Social Security system."* The Interesting aspect is that just a century after Otto von Bismarck introduced his tax-con Biden was advocated adjusting the age to ensure the con continued to provide the Federal Coffers with revenue – the United States life expectancy had reach 74.5 years. Biden backed raising the age and, with an eye toward decreasing them, freezing the benefits.

When there is an elite that views workers as slaves, peons serfs, peasants, or any other term for the lower class menial servants that are easily replaced, the idea of medical care is something that was, when the colonies were formed, outside the economic realm.

We are approaching the end of the history as recognized or defined by Charles Dickens' "Scrooge" when he was told, *"it is more than usually desirable that we should make some slight provision for the Poor and destitute, who suffer greatly at the present time."*

"A Christmas Carol" was published 19 December 1843 and it captured the "*spirit of the times*" or German *zeitgeist*, which is of interest because on 19 June 1843 Karl Marx married a descendant of the 4-Sisters – it was also the year Marx published "*On the Jewish Question*". There is a convergence that we can assert was exactly 44 quadrennial cycles before the 2020 election cycle; if we look at the 48er era Marxist Progressive Liberalism was taking hold in Europe and causing a cultural revolution, three 57-year cycles have passed.

Dickens was addressing things the United States needs to face – America has the largest prison population, and Joe Biden helped create it with the laws he sponsored in 1984, 1986, 1988 and 1994. As Scrooge asked, "*Are there no prisons?*" to which Biden legislation responded: "*Plenty of prisons...*" Of course, there were because the 1984 legislation was accompanied by the emergence of the private prison system which, in 2019, Biden decided he wanted to bring to an end.

In 2019, there were 2.3 million people were in American jails and prisons – 737:100,000 people – about 25% of the world's prison population. Having helped to create the problem, Biden opposed it. Interestingly, one basis for a rising opposition was the investigative reporting by my daughter, Beryl C.D. Lipton, who, as a MuckRock

FOIA editor has spent years at the forefront of revelations about the for-profit prison network.

Dickens even wrote about what we now call "workfare": "*'And the Union workhouses.' demanded Scrooge. 'Are they still in operation?'*"

Dickens has his characters say, "*'Those who are badly off must go there.' ... 'Many can't go there; and many would rather die.' ... 'If they would rather die,' said Scrooge, 'they had better do it, and decrease the surplus population.'*"

Those who deny Universal Health care are simply declaring they would rather see people die or face medical expense poverty, rather than provide the have a healthy and productive society. These death or poverty advocates are part of the Silent and Boomer populations; they have the support of their children, who see it as immoral to adhere to the Good Samaritan role model which does not check the resources of those in need of medical help, but provides it and a recovery period – even if the person in need is wealthy.

Even though Universal Care took hold just 56-57 years after the first American Presidential election, in a society still governed by old people, it takes time. Americans seem to take even longer – but, despite its gerontocracy tendencies, things are changing.

Many will find it hard to accept that the idea of gerontocracy is built into the Constitution – to be a President, a candidate has to be at least 35-years-old. In 1770, when the Founders were drafting the Constitution, they selected what we now know was the average life-span for a European or American. At thirty-five, not only had you outlived half of those born when you were but were also part of a class that had what we call higher education.

Today, an average American or European expects to live till their late seventies or early eighties and that is reflected in the ages of the candidates. By 2030, the Boomer generation will age 65 or older, and five years later, the elderly will, for the first time in the nation's history, comprise over half the population. That means, if no other COVID-19 type virus emerges, the United States will be faced with a population that receiving Social Security and Medicare – with about 20% of the population being workers supporting them.

In my book, "Biblical Prophecy: Are we in the Revelation Era" {AMAZON, March 2014}, I utilized the same 57-period cycle that I use here in terms of quadrennial elections – more accurately, I used the 19-year Metonic sub-cycle of a 57-year astrological period.

There, the focus is on the 19-year period of the Hebrew and Chinese calendars; where western calendar system was created by setting the 198th Metonic cycle to one and justifying it by calling it the birth year of Jesus (even though we know that Jesus had been in Egypt two years before Herod died and that Herod's death is fixed at four years before the start of the western calendar).

In "Biblical Prophecy" the year determining calculations have 2033 as the point associated with the apocalyptic events or the point when we can expect a major war within the context of a third of all life dying – which is consistent with the know extinctions due to both Climate Change and the death of a global Boomer population.

The religious question is also an element of change for this point in time. The prophecy calls for diseases and it would certainly help if they targeted the Baby-Boomers. A global apocalypse is also interesting because it would envision a age where there were World Wars – at a time when half the world had yet to be "discovered".

As of April 2020, the COVID-19 virus offers the media some area of distraction that they can weaponize in their ongoing attacks of Trump. In a perverse way the fact it targets the elderly and infirm can, in terms of future support obligations, be seen as a positive.

As one of the last of the Silent Generation, it seems weird to think of a disease that targets my age group in positive terms, but in economic terms, the choice is the expedited deaths of a generation and its successor generation or a period of longevity in which about 20% of the population is supporting everyone else.

And that being a period when "prophecy" and simple social observation of current events both agree there will be massive social conflict that would, logically, manifest as another World War.

If we think about it, the same population that is supporting 80% of the nation would be the one needed to provide traditional "boot-on-the-ground" troops for that war. OR, maybe, we can mix messages and combine George Orwell's "1984" with The Terminator – released in 1984 – to envision the current world and the mode of warfare that relied on drone, robot, or cyborg technology to fight its wars. It would certainly serve United States interests if Americans could divest themselves from the archaic "boot-on-the-ground" style of foreign intervention and rely more on drones and satellites.

Imagine how weak the United States will be when only a fifth of its population could even be considered for the military, and the real number available for service was less than the 0.5% who were in active service in 2018. Even during the Vietnam draft era, only 2.2% of the population was in military service, and while the 2020 population is 50% larger than it was in 1975 because that was also the beginning of a Baby-Bust, the median age is also 10-years older than it was in 1970 or 1940.

To have a viable military, the population must be healthy.

If or when the current elderly die-off, the population will fall by a third or more. And if those who are left aren't healthy, there will be no military. If the nation fails to establish a Universal Health Care, a World War would require military comprised of Terminators to survive.

In terms of a World War, on 9 March the DJIA opened down, having closed Friday at 25,864.80, on Monday it quickly made a low of 23,754.97 – a drop of 2,109.83 caused by an over the weekend initiation of an oil price war between Russia and Saudi Arabia which saw the price of crude drop 22%.

Underlying the crude oil price war was the virus caused drop in demand caused by decreased tourism negatively impacting airline travel. But the fall in price to the $35 range places it well below the $50 point where, in the United States, it no longer is cost effective to drill for new oil.

The COVID-19 is really exposing things which are far more important than the media focus. Clearly the U.S. needs M4A, but as we see the secondary effects, we learn China provides over 90% of U.S. medications and high tech products a modern society depends on. The oil price shows how critical Russia and China are to fuel supplies needed by the military – think Nazi Germany losing after the Allies cut off its oil and its mechanized forces no longer had fuel.

The virus also exposed the otherwise invisible connections to and countries like Italy and Iran, To get the virus to Iran, there must be human traffic between to two nations – more than between U.S. and China.

CHAPTER ELEVEN **– Nuanced**
"The only thing we did was right
Was the day we started to fight
Keep your eyes on the prize, hold on"
~ Pete Seeger

All things in life involve nuance, some degree of subtle and manipulatable difference that can be spun to mean something that it doesn't by creating a situation where a key portion of assumed knowledge is omitted and the omission debated or ignored.

Nuance is a critical element in negotiation, and those who are failures at negotiating important long-term outcomes are the first to attack and spin things to attack those who are experts in the use or application of nuance.

The beauty of the Trump presidency, the thing that makes it so important as the symbolic start of the new 57 quadrennial cycle in United States history.

As has been pointed out, Trump is in the habit of dropping hints as to what he will accept and the direction he would like things to take. A case in point is when he praised the Australian healthcare system – which would be exceeded by the Progressive M4A if it was constructed in an economically sound manner.

The media and Democrats missed it. They went right passed it, as if he had never said it. However, Tulsi Gabbard, who is the only qualified candidate in the 2020 Democratic field, heard him and, as quoted, went to work developing the plan she called, *"the Single Payer Plus Plan that's loosely modeled after Australia."*

Going into Super Tuesday, Tulsi was sidelined and rendered irrelevant to the nomination process. Afterward, faced with a new primary debate, and the DNC changing the rules to omit her, Tulsi called on former VP Joe Biden and Senator Bernie Sanders to urge the Democratic National Committee (DNC) to allow her onstage.

Tulsi also Tweeted a factor in the biased reality she faced: *"To keep me off the stage, the DNC again arbitrarily changed the debate qualifications. Previously they changed the qualifications in the OPPOSITE direction so Bloomberg could debate. I ask that you stand w/me against the DNC's transparent effort to exclude me from the debates."*

Excluding Tulsi makes sense, in the context of a nomination that has been rigged from the start. We must keep in mind that a primary premise for the impeachment was that Biden – a private citizen when Giuliani compiled and submitted his dossier on Biden's bragging confession to a criminal quid pro quo extortion of foreign officials – was Trump's political rival in the 2020 election.

Without that assertion of a predetermined nomination, the whole argument put forward by Schiff, Nadler, and even Pelosi has no basis. A President has a legal obligation to gather facts related to a public confession of extortion freely offered up by a former elected official – and it is a stronger obligation when they are a former Vice President who implicates a former President as a coconspirator who authorized and would confirm the threat.

Of course, this was made more complicated by the House investigation bring forth the multiple State Department witnesses who asserted Biden's actions were fully consistent with Government Policy. Obama has been silent on the matter. If Biden were simply carrying out Obama era extortion policies, Obama could be called upon to file an affidavit to that effect; Obama would also need to explain the National Interest served by threatening the survival of Ukraine in exchange for the firing of a Prosecutor General.

Obama could simply say he did not authorize or even know of the Biden action. It's an interesting factual nuance which is the difference between Biden having committed a High Crime or simply following a Government Policy set by Obama. It's an interestingly nuanced role for a POTUS who had avoided endorsing his own Vice President – would he accept responsibility for and explain what is, under Federal Law, a crime? Or will he simply allow the false claims that the illegal act has, in some strange and undefined manner, be refuted?

Senator Bernie Sanders pointed out:

"While Sen. Warren and I had nuances of differences – we did – there is no question that her agenda, what she fought for in the campaign, was far closer to what I am fighting for than what Joe Biden believes in."

While speaking in Missouri on 7 March, Biden said:

"If you want a nominee who will bring this party together, who will run a progressive, positive campaign, and turn, turn this primary from a campaign that's about negative attacks

into one that's about what we're for – because we cannot get – re-elect – we cannot win this re-election – excuse me. We can only re-elect Donald Trump – if, in fact, we get engaged in this circular firing squad here. Gotta be a positive campaign, so join us."

Commentators on both the Left and Right looked at these words as muddled to the point that they raised questions about his being mentally fit for the Oval Office. Of course, Trump responded by tweeting, *"I agree with Joe!"*

At a Fox News Town Hall, Trump stated, referring to Biden in the third person:

"I'm all set for Bernie, communist. And then we have this crazy thing that happened on Tuesday, which he thought was Thursday. But he also said 150 million people were killed with guns, and that he was running for the U.S. Senate – there's something going on there."

Pushing Bernie as a communist is Cold War rhetoric aimed at the Baby-Boomers, the younger generation, who are the true base for the Progressive movement, don't make the socialist-communist anti-Russia connection that Boomers were indoctrinated with. But, again, that's part of the nuanced campaign which defines the Trump era.

One nuance factor is the potential for the chosen candidate to maintain an Obama-Trump economy as the demographic controls governing it shift into their next phase. As the readers learned in the previous books in this series, the economic boom economists have been initiated with the market bottom of 2009 was being driven by the demographic realities of 2010.

The Boomer Generation is said to have emerged in 1945, and by 2010 they turned 65-years-old – the traditional age when Social Security benefits are bestowed. When combined with the Baby-Bust that began around 1965 and reached a fertility rate bottom in 2018.

A fertility rate of 2.1 is considered appropriate for population stability; when the rate goes below that, the subject population will grow until the parent generation reaches its life-expectancy limit, at which point the overall population goes into decline.

The fertility rate in Western Europe is about 1.6; about 1.8 in North America; in Sub-Saharan Africa, the 4.6 rate is approximately the global rate in 1950; the current global rate of 2.4 is falling into the negative growth range. With the death of the Baby-Boomers, the global population will plummet.

Population demographics tell us that the number of workers will decline – this is seen in the record high employment rate that Trump boasted of while the Democrats were busy arguing over who would oppose him in November 2020. But who is looking at world events – the events Trump's replacement will need to address when they take office?

Initially, as fertility rates decline, there would be less need for daycare and schools, which frees up both related workers and those who would have been parents to take on other work. As the number of classrooms declines there is a cost-saving for taxpayers. But there is a point where a shrinking working-age population combines with an aging population to render a welfare state unsustainable – unless taxes increase or the elderly die off.

In terms of fatality, the Wuhan virus – otherwise known as COVID-19 or coronavirus – targets the Silent Generation and the oldest members of the Baby-Boom, so we are seeing nature working to achieve that die-off.

In terms of the economy, the Wuhan virus has decimated the Chinese production network which American commerce relies upon and which, after decades of Congress supporting outsourcing, we see Trump working to repatriate so as to make the Western Hemisphere independent of Europe and Asian disruptive forces.

If we look at the side effects, we see curious developments in the area of Medicare for All (M4A) – after the close of the Markets on 10 March, Vice President Pence announced an agreement with private insurance providers to cover costs in the same way Medicare treats the Wuhan virus. This will also eliminate "surprise billing" and add teller-help services of a type already included in Medicare.

Once Wuhan virus changes are integrated into the private medical care system, it should be possible for an intelligent Congress to make them permanent. If that is achieved, the United States can slide into M4A without any viable political opposition – it's hard to oppose what you are already doing profitably, and it is profitable for privatized insurance to offer cost-efficient preventative serves. This is especially true for firms that also provide life insurance – where the longer the client lives, the more the insurer makes.

Other realities are also in play.

Look back at the record decline of the DJIA on 9 March – a price war between two nations the world relies upon for oil triggered a drop in petroleum prices, which then triggered a drop in value for the petroleum industry. For America, there is a net benefit in having lower gas pump and home heating oil prices. But the degree of the extent of the reaction underscores the reliance of fossil fuels which needs to be escaped for National Security reason – yes, there is no question Green Energy needs are important, they make economic sense, and, in the context of Climate Change, make environmental sense. But Green Energy is an economic and national security issue.

If American does not go Green in all things, the United States will become dependent on the Middle East and Russia for energy. During the Second World War, severing Nazi Germany from its Middle Eastern petroleum supplier brought their mechanized forces to screeching halt and resulted in abandoned tanks and trucks. The United States is, as of 2018, one of the three largest oil producers in the world. But its oil is shale oil – that is, it represents the scraping of the bottom of the figurative barrel of oil wells that were once seen as "gushers" but are now pumped dry of the free-flowing liquid.

With the price war, crude prices dropped by 22%-25%. That fall brought the price at least $13 below a breakeven point for shale oil production – which explains devaluation of stocks in that sector.

As cited in previous books in this series, we already know the military has moved to green applications to replace those now in use based on fossil fuels. The effect has resulted in significant advances in military communications and positioning capability.

In New Hampshire on 29 December 2019, Joe Biden was asked what would happen *"If we don't stop using fossil fuels–"* ... he didn't even allow the question to be completed before saying, *"We're all dead."*

As Biden told his audience: *"We have to set sort of guide rails down now, so between the years 2021 and 2030, it's irreversible – the path we set ourselves on. And one of which is doing away with any substance for fossil fuels – number one."*

Biden was focused, as Sanders was, on Global Warming and general Climate Change. But realistically, that is out of the control of a humanity which became devoted to the industrial revolution before there was a United States. The United States is a guidepost for the Industrial Revolution and the evolution of Climate Change

– and it took over 60 quadrennial cycles for humanity to grasp what it had created and humanity has to realize that it should go with the flow and not against it.

The Russians and Saudis each want some degree of control or dominance over oil, but fossil fuels are on the way out – or should be for any advanced nation interested in its national security.

Throughout the first three years of the Trump administration OPEC and Russia have cooperated to support the market, and they joined efforts to stabilize prices to mitigate the economic impact of the coronavirus outbreak. But, in March, OPEC (the Organization of the Petroleum Exporting Countries), proposed production cuts and Russia declined cooperation – an act that might relate to the failed attempt in the last two years of the Obama Administration to squeeze out United States production which under Trump grew into the world's biggest oil producer by doubling shale oil production.

Throughout the Trump era, we have heard persistent mantras related to "Russia, Russia, Russia" in connection with covert moves to influence the elections. But the reality of propaganda has them simply making derogatory assertions on some social media platform – these can be against Trump, connecting him to a false or blatantly silly premise for another impeachment or accusations of treason and incompetence. Assert incompetence and some Never Trump pundit in the MSM will pounce on as a background premise some assertion they can later ignore having ever made.

Vladimir Putin is aware that much of America's economy is predicated on debt – President Trump knows this and consistently pushes for lower interest rates – and debt is leverage which, when it can be undermined can render an industry or economy fragile in terms of outside agent attacks.

By increasing supply, in an economic environment of steady demand, the price of oil falls below the economically sustainability of the American or Canadian fracking industry and can cripple the debt-fueled growth which allowed America to become the world's largest oil producer. If the American fracking industry crumbles, it will be Russia that grabs market share through geographic location and control of territory carrying pipelines to Europe and Asia.

To counter Russia, Saudi Arabia must increase production and drive prices below levels Russian production costs can sustain.

Comically, this enhances American oil-based industries and makes anything that is petroleum-dependent cheaper. That bolsters the record Obama-Trump economic growth, and, if Congress shows some degree of intelligence, allows both time economic resources to transition to a green economy that Russia can no longer influence.

Many people know the Supply and Demand Curve, but ignore the reality that it is a Supply, Demand, Cost, Need Curve. And Need is related to Usefulness – which involves both daily practicalities and incorporates a degree of physical and emotional factors.

Food is useful but also necessary – at least to the extent that we must have the nutrients it provides. But we can get those nutrients from a meal, or a tablet, or intravenous (like a hospital coma patient).

Everything in life involved nuance or variables which go deeper and deeper into dictating the behavior of all matter until there is a point where "choice" ceases to be a factor; even then, nuance asserts the argumentative existence of choice.

Go to the elemental atomic level and you find electrons revolving around a nucleus in the way a planet revived around the sun. Kick the electron free and it will travel until it finds a neutron to either revolve around or crash into. Maybe it crashes into another electron that's revolving around that neutron, or into a proton of equal strength and they become a neutron.

A meteor crashes into a sun or planet or approaches at the precise speed and angle to be caught in the gravitational field and enter orbit as a planet or moon – as an electron, the orbital action creates a new element, while the impact can cause a nuclear reaction or explosion.

Everything is the same, only different; everything's the same, only the order of magnitude changes. The order of magnitude came to be a mathematical constant, or it can be called the nuance.

When we hear talk of a Trade War or tariffs, it could be taking basic supply and demand then tossing in a tax.

Governments need taxes to pay for services. True, they print money, but the money only has meaning if it has value and it only has value if it can serve as a substitute for direct barter of products and services. And money can be created without government intervention through the existence and use of CREDIT: the promise to pay or provide a product or service, at a later date.

Both money and credit are the same -- they represent a symbol of trust between individuals as managed or guaranteed by a third party entity.

A tariff is a tax, it's also a service charge related to the use of a border or the right to engage in commerce across a border. Internally, between States or communities, a sales tax can be seen as a tariff. At one level, it's a source of revenue for the government in which people decide to pay when the decision to buy a product or chose between basically identical products having different prices. On another level, the fee, sales tax, or tariff can serve as a deterrent targeting a specific product or service.

Vary the cost and you can alter the demand which can affect the supply. But the relationship works in many ways. If you have a steady demand, you can reduce the supply and that raises the cost. If the demand is variable, supply and cost must be balanced in a way to maximize profit by meeting an average level of demand.

Trigger an emotional component and you can control the demand -- increasing it or decreasing it based on which supply/demand/cost variable you want to control.

Emotional control is called advertising, propaganda, or "word of mouth" (gossip).

Since people need to be part of the herd or be seen as leaders of the herd (trendsetters), the sales pitch is either "everyone's doing it" or "this is what everyone will be doing -- so be the first". Done properly, there is no need for proof, there is only the logic behind THE EMPEROR'S NEW CLOTHES and wanting to see what other's cannot, if only because it supposedly proved you're smarter than they are, or are part of the elite class who do see something others cannot.

The quote from the Pete Seeger song has deep roots in older songs and quotes that reach back to Luke 9:62: "*No one who puts a hand to the plow and looks back is fit for service in the kingdom of God*"; the idea is to keep your eyes and mind on the task in front of you. But the Biblical analogy has a flaw – when you plow, you want the furrows to be straight and orderly so, even now and then, you need to look back.

It's a subtle nuance. While keeping the eye on the prize, you also need to check your work and confirm you are still on course – but you must always keep your mind's eye on the prize.

On the day after the South Carolina caucus, the Democratic field had been reduced to five candidates; three of them – Gabbard, Warren, and Biden – are descendants of the 4-Sisters and so are direct descendants of Charlemagne. Two candidates, Klobuchar and Buttigieg, gave their pre-Super Tuesday endorsement to Joe Biden who said he would raise taxes on anyone who "*benefitted*" from the Trump tax cuts.

Beforer to his South Carolina caucus defeat, Pete Buttigieg took a shot at Sanders which also backhanded Bloomberg: "*I don't want our nominee, to have House Democrats stuck explaining why we nominated Bernie Sanders when we could have nominated a Democrat.*"

Sanders is not a Democrat, the Democratic Party has not yet caught up with him or the 170-year old Progressive movement he has re-energized and re-vitalized. He is also the enemy of all those who demonizes four-letter words ... like LOVE or LIKE. Sanders is one who promotes the premise underlying The Good Samaritan; he certainly someone the far-Right would oppose. But that doesn't say Sanders is presidential material, though it would make him an ideal Senate Majority Leader.

On 7 March Bernie Sanders Tweeted:

"My Republican friends tell us the only way we can 'strengthen Social Security' is, in fact, to cut Social Security.

"Nonsense!

'Seniors cannot make it on $13,000 a year. When we talk about strengthening Social Security, that means increasing benefits, not cutting them."

On 10 March, Trump invoked the Wuhan virus as an excuse to promote eliminating payroll taxes for the remaining nine months of 2020 – bringing an end to the cash flow which has supported the pay-as-you-go Social Security system and Medicare. By so doing, he would allow Congress the opportunity to deprive the government of an estimated $700 billion in cash flow.

At the same time, Trump suggested Congress should consider a Petroleum Industry bailout to offset further Russian undermining of oil prices.

Fiscally, the two proposals are an idealized version of the Far-Right Reaganomics that created the humongous National Debt and threatens the National survival after 2035.

Anyone pushing for cuts to the income of roughly 30-percent of their nation is seeking to crash the economy and cause a massive increase in welfare dependence. Proponents of Reaganomics and outsourcing knew this. Under Reagan, Republicans the expression, "A rising tide lifts all boats," was integral to the propaganda selling points used to transfer wealth to the 1-percent – the implication being they were the tide, when, in truth, it was a ploy to allow them to exit the harbor, so they could relocate their business to China and return that empire to its traditional mercantile dominance.

It was a simple analogy: tidewater comes in below the hull, from beneath the hull; the tide then lifts larger ships whose size has them grounded on the harbor bottom.

Economically this is achieved by lifting the wages of the poor – or so the ignorant masses believed. But what the common folk failed to realize is small boats seldom run aground. It is only the massive merchant vessel that experiences difficulty in shallow water.

Economically, shallow water is low or below poverty income.

We know this, and hear it in association with the expression: "*Give a man a fish and you feed him for a day; teach a man to fish and you feed him for a lifetime.*" Various third world "seed money" programs are based on this adage.

Those who attack Sanders for being a Democratic Socialist are most certainly ignorant of or opposed to, the Bible where we are told: "..., *but rather let him labor, doing honest work with his own hands, so that he may have something to share with anyone in need.*" {Ephesians 4:28} While the verse deals with someone not being forced to steal to survive, the key element is that you work so you can help those in need.

In Marxism, the Bible verse comes across as having "surplus capital" that will then be used for the general good. In the capitalist context, we have public services and only issue is one of definition – M4A should be defined as a basic necessary public service that is already provided, on a limited basis, by emergency medical units.

Trump appears to have taken the position of undermining the economy and national survival, but will a President Biden provide anything beneficial?

The 7 November 1972 Senatorial election was when Joseph Biden qualified to go to Washington; two weeks later he turned thirty and he has been there, voting on everything, ever since.

On 21 February 1972, Richard Nixon went to China, setting the stage for the December 1978 announcement, by Deng Xiaoping, of an Open Door Policy toward any foreign business wishing to avail itself of a market comprising a sixth of the global population.

Given it had cheap labor and a traditionally well-educated population, outsourcing allowed China to first step back on the global merchant stage. Thus, by 2013 President Xi Jinping in a position to announce the creation of a trade corridor between China and its neighbors in the west which was dubbed "The New Silk Road".

Reaganomics encouraged outsourcing which didn't just ship business to China, it removed tax revenues and employment in what were once critical parts of the manufacturing sector. The United States lost its self-sufficient character and was reduced to being a service industry nation whose balance of trade profits were derived from agriculture.

During this period, Trump was focused on turning the family-based residential apartment business in New York's outer boroughs into an international real estate business. His daughter Ivanka was born nine months after the dawn of the Reagan era and was elected to the board of *100 Women in Hedge Funds* nine months before President Xi Jinping gave his speech, "*Promote People-to-People Friendship and Create a Better Future*", in which he announced the New Silk Road proposal.

What were the Bidens doing during this timeframe?

We know the rising tide concept was keyed to "*Trickle Down Economics*" – the idea that you pour the water into the top and then it overflows to lift the other boats. But, for trickle down to trickle down, the hulls of the larger vessels must be filled – capsizing or sinking many vessels. Naturally, the large vessels leave with their hulls full and then sell contents in distant ports – they outsource.

Voters understand that "trickle-down economics" is nonsense and destroys an economy while creating Michael Bloomberg type billionaires whose wealth comes from creating ever-larger buckets in which to collect the downpour.

Cutting payroll taxes might sound good, and adds a small boost to the take-home pay of those accustomed to paying the tax throughout the year, and fits the trickle-down model. But, if Social

Security is frozen or cut, a third of the adult population is denied the purchasing power that supports small businesses.

Denied disposable income or the ability to save, the elderly lose their value in maintaining the economy – without the spending of those who are retired, there is no economic base or foundation upon which every healthy the economy relies.

Moreover, if they cannot meet expenses, welfare supplements their income, which means several dollars of increased cost for every dollar cut. As it is, the Russian oil price war has had the effect of lowering the value of the financial markets. That means nothing unless you have a 401k or other retirement fund that relies either on interest and dividends or just on capital appreciation.

There was a time when Real Estate had value. But the Wuhan virus targets the elderly populations who are the largest segment of the demographic segment now occupying the homes sitting of that real property. When they die, there will be an overabundance of housing and market values should fall while new home construction ceases to have meaning.

The nuance lies in Climate Change – the flooding of shoreline property and the creation of Climate Refugees, which will drive the population inland and north to what are now rural areas with an overabundance of vacant properties. Interestingly, these are the same rural areas where Green Energy has gained prominence – so those who move into rural areas will also be moving into a green economy culture where the only thing currently lacking is reliable and appropriate wireless communication. And, by appropriate, I mean reliable high-speed telecommuting capability.

Climate Change and whatever follow the Wuhan coronavirus are coming together to fulfill prophecy for those who believe in such things – a third of life shall die by 2050 and the world will be reborn into an interdependent global economy. The only thing the United States is deciding is its place in that new world.

While decisions were being made, on 20 March, the Canadian and Mexican-American borders were closed to nonessential traffic; the week closed with the DJIA down at 19,173.98; media reports had begun claiming China covered-up the true extent of their Wuhan problem; while in Italy 627 people died in the previous twenty-four hours, while by mid-night on the 20th, a total of 242 Americans had died since the first death on 29 February.

CHAPTER TWELVE – FUN BEGINS

"Our future remains brighter than anyone can imagine. Acting with compassion and love, we will heal the sick, care for those in need, help our fellow citizens, and emerge from this challenge stronger and more unified than ever before." ~ Donald J. Trump, 11 March 2020

Throughout the past seven books in the series, we looked at Trump's approach to government and have seen him treat it the same way a businessman specializing in Real Estate would approach any market that needs what they had to offer.

From their inception, the American Colonies or the United States of America have served as a mercantile catalyst driving the globalization of industrial development. Given the history of slavery and racism that is so easily associated with the evolution and then the emergence of modern nations, there is a disinclination to think in terms of America's role as a global force in the development of trade – a role historically associated with the spice Trade and ancient Silk Road generally referred to in terms of Marco Polo and his career between 1271 and 1295.

After Marco Polo, we are taught to think in terms of Spain, France, and England competing for "newly discovered territories" – Western territories the Vikings {793–1066} had reached centuries earlier. Then there is the eventual dominance of the British Empire – the last European Empire ruled by descendants of the 4-Sisters who were descendants of Charlemagne {768–814} and the Normans who were Vikings who settled in northern France until 1066 when they conquered the southern region of the island territories whose northern regions were already occupied by their kinsmen.

If we go back to the time of Julius Caesar, we find China was providing silks and spices to the Roman Empire, and Britain was the land where its seamen could sail against the wind. Driven north by Roman forces, those seamen eventually became Vikings and, as the Normans, reclaimed the territories the Romans had conquered – by attacking from the same direction or route Caesar had taken nearly eleven centuries earlier.

As we know, in 1492, it was Spanish ships that sailed west in hopes of reaching China and establishing a sea-based route for the lucrative Asian trade. But, in the period between July and August

1588, British seamanship again showed itself to be as meaningful and skilled a force as Caesar acknowledged, and history details how the Spanish Armada was defeated by the more maneuverable and swifter British ships – now more formidable than Viking longboats that established Atlantic-Mediterranean and Varangian trade routes seven-centuries earlier.

In *"Grandpa Was Deity"* you leaned that yDNA revealed the connection between the Indus Valley, and every culture recognized to have shaped modern civilization. That shaping has now resulted in China versus the United States as merchants to the world. The role the United States assumed 400-years ago as shipbuilder to the world – a trade facilitator whose function was augmented by cotton and tobacco. And then there was the slave trade captured in the musical, *"1776"*: "... *Molasses to rum to slaves / 'Tisn't morals, 'tis money that saves / Shall we dance to the sound of a profitable pound / In molasses and rum and slaves..."*

The "Triangle Trade" which emerged when hackmatack or tamarack trees – more properly called Larix laricina, or American larch – whose trunk and root structure made them ideal for creating a single piece continuous bow and keel that ideal for the design of the sturdy merchant vessels, the "tall ships," that would command global trade routes for over two-hundred-fifty years.

Of course, as in Europe, China, Korea, and Japan constitute a commonly derived and inter-related network that splintered into semi-isolated and specialized tribal groups. China is the mercantile culture that invented toilet paper and paper currency – and there must be a relevant joke buried in there.

If we look at Indo-European culture, the common origin lays in genetics – the yDNA haplogroup combination of R1a and R1b that defines the Brahmin of India, Ashkenazi Hebrew, and Vikings. R1b is the Atlantic modal haplotype found in France and presumably linked to Charlemagne, who was the founder of the European royals and is the ancestor to all US Presidents.

History has a perverse sense of humor. It sets in motion the thing which gives rise to prophesy. Charlemagne was born in the year 748; twenty years later he was King of the Franks; six years after that, he was King of the Lombards – according to Wikipedia, *"the Lombards descended from a small tribe called the Winnili, who dwelt in southern Scandinavia"* from whence came the Vikings during the 790s when Charlemagne's Carolingian Empire was born.

Why the history lesson? Where is the fun in the emergence of a European Empire around the time when the first millennium is ending?

Part of the "humor" is the persistent parallels. Charlemagne was, and through his descendants remains, a key figure in western history; in the current environment, the Lombard region of Italy is among the top locations for the COVID-19 outbreak – why? What is the link between Lombard-Italy and Wuhan-China?

The Carolingian Empire was overlapped by the Tang Dynasty which is considered a high point in Chinese cosmopolitan culture – traditional woodblock printing was moving toward the development of moveable type, and the mercantile culture was highly lucrative. The earliest example of woodblock print books was under Empress Shōtoku, who reigned between 749 and 770 – the period in which Charlemagne born and came into power. It would be almost 700-years before Johannes Gutenberg would introduce the first movable type printing system into Germany.

Why a history lesson on parallel cultures that have yet to lose their fundamental characters? Could it be that it took 700-years for a basic scholarly technology to travel 8200 km (5100 miles)?

There was a fundamental similarity between the two cultures. Under the Tang Dynasty, the day-to-day governance was conducted by civil servants who were scholars. Under Charlemagne, scholars were also prized and their origin was the Kingdom of Northumbria in a region once marked by Hadrian's Wall – the southern boundary of what would eventually be the Viking territories which would see a Viking merchant-scholar class occupy Northumbria.

That was 1250 years ago and there is a relationship between East and West in which the East was the dominant mercantile power – much as it is today. And Charlemagne gave rise to a written script known as Carolingian minuscule which approximates our lower case letters. But, in that period scholarship in Europe was secondary to militarism; the parallels between China and America can be seen as similar due to the huge military budget the United States has chosen to maintain, while China is creating a millionaire mercantile class.

To date, it appears Charlemagne is the common ancestor to every American President – the exception is Martin Van Buren, for whom there is insufficient ancestral history to affirm his inclusion. But he would also the ancestor to all the European Kings.

For our purposes, we come forward nine generations to his 7th great-grandson, William the Conqueror who would establish, in 1066, the Viking-Franc Nobility who are now represented by Queen Elizabeth's royal family. While it took time for the invasion to take control, within thirty years the University of Oxford (1096) came into existence; when their descendants landed in Plymouth (1620), it only took fifteen years for them to establish Harvard (1636).

From William, we come forward four more generations to the 5th Earl of Chester, Hugh Gernon of Cyfeiliog, whose daughters are the 4-Sisters whose connections to the various Presidents are shown on the back cover of this book.

The 19 or 57 quadrennial periods referred to are historical units connected to major stones at Stonehenge which, among other things, predict eclipses. The 19-year periods that are represented by the 56-stones (a 19, 19, 18 count) at Stonehenge, became the basis for the Hebrew, Chinese, and Runic calendars are all the same 19-year Metonic cycle; even our modern western calendar is derived from this system.

At the request of the Pope, who sought to align the holidays of Passover and Easter, a Scythian monk named Dionysius Exiguus (Dennis the Humble) reset the 198th node of the Hebrew calendar to one and called it the Year of Christ's birth – with improvements, the world is using that ancient that is tied to the Chinese. In *"Grandpa Was a Deity"*, the yDNA line traced revealed they were Brahmin, Hebrew, and the proto-Vikings who would settle Iceland and be the first to land in America – bringing back Native American women who became their wives and provide the maternal line of the Icelandic population (established by their mtDNA).

Fun: History has served to move the symmetrical alignment between east and west to the New World where it became the United States just as America moved through 57 quadrennial periods. It's also the point in religious history when the biblical prophecy is supposed to come into play.

The fun is, we are no longer supposed to accept the ancient religions, so have a divide between the Right-wing evangelicals and secularist culture that strips away the mystical aspects of *"Grandpa Was A Deity"* – that the *"men of renown"* leaders, who ruled before the mythical Flood, still rule as religious icons. Before the Romans could replace their *"men of renown"* deities, to be more noteworthy than the grandchildren of a deity, it was necessary to elevate Jesus to an exalted status as the *"only begotten son"* {John 3:16} of the primary deity and a human female.

What we strip away the mystical, we find science and math of a type that is highly important today. The fun part is the prophecy – there is no logical explanation for why such long-term predictions of events should appear to work. Yet, as was presented in *"Biblical Prophecy: Are we in the Revelation Era"*, it appears that Metonic cycles are the basis for the dating of events that were supposed to occur in our era – and, if Hitler was the White Horseman, the events seem to be playing out on schedule. If that's the case, then Climate Change and the death of the Baby-Boomer generation were integral to the final stages – with the Wuhan virus targeting that generation.

On 15 March, the Sanders-Biden Democratic Debate was held without an audience; having closed at 23,185.60 on Friday, Monday, 16 March, saw the DJIA register a record one day fall of 2,997.10 to close at 20,188.52, having set a 52-week low at 20,116.46 or about 32% below its 52-week high.

Over the past forty years, various scientific papers have been written about the relationship between animals and human health. As we know, the Old Testament dietary laws forbid the consumption of certain creatures, the most commonly mentioned being pork – even contact with pigs is deemed unclean.

In ancient times, before the era of Moses, there were cultures where pork was avoided and individuals associated with swine were segregated as "unclean." Many would recognize this as the Indian caste system where we find the "Untouchable" class who "consume life" – they aren't vegetarians consistent with the commandment to Adam & Eve in Genesis 1:29, *"Behold, I have given you every plant yielding seed that is on the face of all the earth and every tree with seed in its fruit."*

As I've done in other books, we can see the transition to our carnivore diet – there is a point with Abram & Sarah where milk and meat are consumed, but by the time of Moses we find they realized it was unwise to eat anything that died a "natural" death – died of an unknown cause – and that we *"shalt not seethe a kid in his mother's milk"* {Deut 14:21}. Obviously, the rule is not to boil or cook, but a sense of caution elevated it to not having the two as part of the same meal. Today, your doctor might place you on a healthy diet that is, on multiple levels, what we might recognize as a "kosher" diet – if we compared it to the biblical guidelines.

For our purposes, the issue revolves around pork.

In ancient Greece, the Scythians were called "the wisest of men" and they forbid pigs in their eastern steppe territory. There are genetic studies that relate the Scythian to the Indus Valley yDNA and establish them as part of the Indo-European culture reflected in both the Hindu and Hebrew dietary traditions.

Today we associate pork fat with clogged arteries and heart disease. But few people are aware of the flu research stating, "*Asian flu in 1957, Hong Kong flu in 1968, and "Russian" flu in 1977 -- also have been traced to traditional Chinese agricultural practices.*" In those "*agricultural practices,*" we can identify the organic Petri dish environment in which creates the type of virus which we later see as the basis for a pandemic.

In a 2001 article in The Blade, science editor Michael Woods wrote: "*Pigs shuffle the genes of human and bird flu viruses like two decks of playing cards. It creates the new strains of influenza that march around the globe each year like an invading army.*"

In The Pediatric Infectious Disease Journal: November 2005, doctors Kahn and McIntosh stated:

"While research was proceeding to explore the pathogenicity and epidemiology of the human coronaviruses, the number, and importance of animal coronaviruses were growing rapidly. Coronaviruses were described that caused disease in multiple animal species, including rats, mice, chickens, turkeys, calves, dogs, cats, rabbits and pigs."

It is well established that Canine coronavirus disease, known as CCoV, is a highly infectious intestinal infection in dogs, and that is NOT related to the virus which causes the COVID-19 Wuhan virus – but there is a suspicion that there is a bat-related version that is a relative of the Wuhan virus.

The origins of Wuhan coronavirus are currently unknown but they are a class of Human coronaviruses which were first discovered in 1965 and named B814. The discovery was first characterized in a 1966 *Lancet* article "*Cultivation of viruses from a high proportion of patients with colds*', published by virologists Tyrrell and Bynoe.

Subsequent data indicated up to 35% of the total respiratory viral activity during epidemics was associated with coronavirus infections. With the Wuhan virus, we see a virus that has evolved to the point where it is only lethal in people who suffer other forms of respiratory distress – or, as in the case of health care workers, where the respiratory system is overburdened with slightly different forms of coronavirus carrying "contaminants" from multiple prior hosts.

Originally it was observed that, like many other respiratory viruses, an infection could occur at any age, but it was most common in children and reinfection was common. But, the 1965 discovery infers a post-Baby-Boomer variation or disease which the younger generation would develop an immunity to that could then be passed to their children. As a result, the Baby-Boom and Silent Generation are the ones with no immunity.

Dr. Kenneth McIntosh concluded the 2005 article with the statement:

"Theoretically, if you took a virus like RSV or parainfluenza and introduced it for the first time into the human population, adults, who are infected and have no preexisting immunity, might develop more severe disease than babies. However, until further research can verify this, it can only be seen as a theory."

Fifteen years later, what was theoretical during the Bush-era had become established fact in the Trump era. A version of Human parainfluenza viruses (HPIVs) which commonly caused respiratory illnesses in infants and young children affects their grandparents to a far greater extent.

Wuhan virus has confirmed the McIntosh speculation.

The emergence of the Wuhan virus has served to create the exact conditions to justify initiating the Progressive agenda Bernie Sanders has promoted throughout his adult life. It has also exposed the weaknesses that have been cited in my books for over a decade.

In April 2019, Brent Crude was 74.04; on 19 March 2020, it was at 30.03 and, as this book was being edited, gasoline at my local Irving station was $1.73/gal – the lowest it has been in years.

As the process of dealing with the domestic spread of Wuhan virus increased the need for bureaucratic management, Trump used a standard business response – delegating acquisition of long-term equipment needs to the states, telling the governors: *"Respirators, ventilators, all of the equipment — try getting it yourselves. We will be backing you, but try getting it yourselves. Point of sales, much better, much more direct if you can get it yourself."*

Expedite purchases; expedite treatment; improve outcomes.

As Trump explained it to the reporters:

"If they can get them faster by getting them on their own, in other words, go through a supply chain that they may have, because … during normal times, the governors buy a lot of things not necessarily through federal government.

"It's always going to be faster if they can get them directly, if they need them, and I've given them authorization to order directly."

Trump has exercised a similar approach to delegating actions when, on 13 March, he announced the federal government would cut red tape, clearing a way for safe, effective, convenient and affordable community testing for the coronavirus by facilitating an ability for pharmacies to provide services within the scope of their function as accessible health care providers.

In that role, they would partner with other frontline providers of health care, thereby advancing health and wellness, while also reducing the need for doctor, clinic or hospital visits. It's well established that 95-percent of Americans live within five miles of a retail pharmacy which can seamlessly and efficiently adjust services to provide coronavirus testing.

When the private sector units with government to innovate problem-solving, they can produce solutions that achieve a common good. But to do so, the naysayers – the Swamp Denizens who have assumed the role of Never-Trumpers – must be neutralized. The importance of this is seen in their reaction to Trump authorizing the States to utilize their acquisition resources to expedite necessary medical upgrades.

The Never-Trump types jumped on the statement, reducing it to a caustic "Trump tells states, 'get it yourself'" style remark. But for the Federal government to buy the equipment, then get it where it's needed, require a duplicating the purchasing network already in place within the states. The result would be unnecessary delays and loss of life caused by the states effectively outsourcing the needs of their residents to a Federal bureaucracy.

However, Bernie Sanders has used his campaign to point out the national health danger created by over four decades of private sector outsourcing: *"It is incomprehensible that we are dependent on China and other countries for masks, for prescription drugs, for* rubber gloves, and for key parts needed to make advanced medical equipment."

On 11 March, Ted Cruz showed that Sanders' viewpoint had become bipartisan: *"This is a serious problem. As the current crisis illustrates, we should NOT be dependent on China for life-saving medicines. We can't keep giving China that economic/military weapon. We need domestic capacity, made in the USA, to protect American lives."*

A variation on the fossil fuel energy dangers we've alluded to throughout this book series was raised by Rosemary Gibson, author of *"China Rx: Exposing the Risks of America's Dependence on China for Medicine"* and senior adviser with the Hastings Center stated: *"If China shut the door on exports of core components to make our medicines, within months our pharmacy shelves would become bare and our health care system would cease to function."*

Yanzhong Huang, a senior fellow for global health with the Council on Foreign Relations, Chinese pharmaceutical companies are supplying 70% of acetaminophen, 40-45% of heparin, vitamin C, ibuprofen, hydrocortisone and over 90% of the antibiotics many Americans depend on. Trump has been trying to repatriate a wide range of outsourced industries, presumably Wuhan virus will ensure Big Pharma is alerted to the need to comply with his objective.

Wuhan virus obviously created a disruptive element for the global economic environment. But it has also initiated forces that should promote the Progressive movement which has been slowly evolving since the 1840s program – a movement which, during the 2016 and 2020 campaigns has become associated with both Bernie Sanders and Alexandria Ocasio-Cortez.

Of course, Universal Healthcare or M4A is an obvious aspect that is being introduced with "temporary" changes to the Medicare and ACA system coordination with the private sector. But we also have the idea of a Universal Basic Income (UBI) that gained strength when President Trump floated the idea of a payroll tax holiday, then shifted toward the more immediate action of injecting cash into the American wallet faster than drip-drip of a payday where take-home cash is increased by only 6.3%.

As Trump said: *"I think we are going to do something that gets money to them as quickly as possible. We will have a pretty good idea at the end of the day what we will be doing."*

Republican Senator Mitt Romney proposed giving every adult $1,000 to help meet any financial needs created by the mandatory closure of various businesses where large numbers of people gather. And in keeping with the bipartisan approach, Representative Ilhan Omar suggested providing $1,000 to every adult, and an additional $500 per child.

By 10:30 AM on 18 March, the House and Senate passed first stage legislation was on its way to Trump for his signature. There is clear evidence that the pandemic has served an important social role by showing Americans that they need to return to their roots – the rugged individualism of the "Old West" is less important than the group collectivism that gave us "Barn Raising" gatherings; health – be it physical or economic – is dependent on those around us. We need Universal Healthcare to keep families alive and to keep those upon whom we rely in good health.

After the vote, Bernie Sanders tweeted the motivation for his colleagues: "*I voted for this coronavirus bill, a step in the right direction. As Congress drafts new legislation, we must go much further. For example, we need free health care and paid sick leave for all. Our job is to protect, at all cost, the health and economic safety of every American.*"

After decades of bailing out the wealthy elite, government has been given clear evidence that it is the poorest among us who need to be focused on. One would suspect Right-wing evangelicals would understand: "*The poor you will always have with you, but you will not always have Me.*" (Matt 26:11) In American today, citizens do not need to be poor, UBI is not a handout, it is a national economic foundation that supports people in times of a pandemic and foreign acts of economic or military self-service like the Russia-Saudi oil price war. Of course, that price war could well benefit America with lower energy costs while Wuhan virus has suppressed incomes.

The pandemic will reveal Trump's true business intelligence.

About 108-years-ago, Theodore Roosevelt, a Republican, ran as a Progressive promoting healthcare. In Europe, France, Britain, and Germany already had programs that helped their citizens stave off the financial difficulty. The cause underlying nature and causes of the problems did not matter – unemployment, injury, old age, illness, or the breadwinner's death – they only needed to live, to be a part of the human experience. These programs were not a bailout for risk-takers of those who made poor business decisions, or some level of a greedy elite.

Twenty-three years later, The Great Depression provided the foundation upon which Franklin Delano Roosevelt was able to build Social Security and then came Medicaid/Medicare. Wuhan virus is serving as the foundation for appropriate preparation for a Climate Change era in which there will be new never before seen diseases.

In voting on the legislation, Republican Senator John Thune said: *"I don't think anybody's looking at it in terms of bailouts. I think we're looking at what does it take to keep critical industries and small businesses afloat."* Part of keeping businesses afloat was ensuring their customers could remain, customers, as the nation moves toward what some say is a recession and others are seeing as a possible depression brought on by a pandemic that could last 18-months or longer.

The Main Stream Media (MSM) initially grabbed the Wuhan virus as its new prime focus for attacking the administration while also ignoring solutions presented by Bernie Sanders and the call for M4A.

In a statement published on 10 March, Harvard University President Lawrence S. Bacow said:

"Despite our best efforts to bring the University's resources to bear on this virus, we are still faced with uncertainty - and the considerable unease brought on by uncertainty. It will take time for researchers, a good many of them who are our colleagues, to understand enough about this disease to mount a reliable defense against it. Now more than ever, we must do our utmost to protect those among us who are most vulnerable, whether physically or emotionally, and to treat one another with generosity and respect."

The context of his comment was the announcement Harvard was canceling classes and shifting to virtual class attendance, with the added request that students on Spring Break do not return to the campus. In addition, all "non-essential" gatherings of more than 25 people were being discouraged.

On the same day, Bernie Sanders announced his decision to cancel a campaign rally which already had over five thousand people who had registered their plan to attend. Thus the Wuhan virus had begun to reshape the campaigns for Sanders and Biden – where the day before Biden had held a campaign rally where he shook hands with attendees.

It then became important to recognize the one in six of those who contract the virus and are in the age range of Biden and Sanders die. Overall, the Wuhan fatality rate is one or two percent, but it is skewed to the elderly and those with underlying medical conditions – many of which would not exist if the nation had a M4A system and an Obamacare system devoid of the private insurer component in which there is a prohibitive co-pay component that discourages early preventative health care measures.

In a 31 January speech, Joe Biden attacked Trump for his ban on China travel – labeling it "fear-mongering," adding that *This is no time for … hysteria and xenophobia – hysterical xenophobia."* But, by 18 March, affected nations had closed their borders – the US-Canadian border was closed by Canada – and people were being told to "shelter in place" and practice "social distancing". Would a POTUS Biden have delayed travel restrictions for seven weeks or engaged in any of the now proven significant preventative actions taken by Trump? Would Canada have had to close its border before Biden would stop travel from China or Europe?

On 12 March, Biden accused anyone using the term Wuhan virus as being "xenophobic," which seems to deny the reality of the Wuhan coronavirus having origins – or making its first appearance – in the Wuhan region of China. Certainly, the virus doesn't identify with a race or nationality, it only evolves where it evolves. And that is the problem soon to be associated with climate change-related diseases.

Biden lied or misrepresented reality when, in February, he said, "*…with Ebola – I was part of making sure that pandemic did not get to the United States, saved millions of lives."*

This man, who would wait for the last minute to halt travel from infected regions – he would not name because its "xenophobic" to identify regions dominated by other races, or maybe it's just that Biden has been a staunch supporter of China since 2013 when they gave Hunter Biden a $1.5 Billion deal.

It seems comical, after denouncing Trump for the travel ban initiated in the middle of January, and formalized on the 31st, the media attacked Trump for not having instituted travel bans earlier – like the Middle Eastern ban, stopping those with Iranian contact.

Cognitive dysfunction seems to prevail. While we have calls for "social distancing" while "sheltering-in-place", the media was showing images from Florida, where thousands were going to the beach. At the same time, MSM was challenging a seeming priority that saw tests given to professional athletes and others whose work brings them into contact with crowds – where they could serve as "typhoid Mary" type asymptomatic carriers.

Logically, MSM attacks were on Biden's opposition to travel bans. But, the pundits could not make the connection. As a result, we can expect support for Biden and policies that would be deadly to Americans – even while the real legislative direction has turned to that advocated by Sanders throughout his political career and by Progressives since the 1840s. If we push reality, these are policies that Evangelicals should have been supporting Progressive programs as a secular variation on words attributed to Jesus in the New Testament.

However, whatever Sanders is promoting can only achieve success if Trump decides he wants a Presidential Status to rival FDR – in which case, he will see how the Coronavirus Legislation works and then improve upon it as his new Progressive platform presented as a Conservative approach to building national security in the face of future threats.

In three primaries held on 17 March, across-the-board Biden defeated Sanders by 2:1 – as a result, Biden should have sufficient delegates to secure him the nomination and make him the political rival that Schiff and rest of those promoting Trump's impeachment had stated he would be from the moment he announced in 2018.

In December 2019, Tulsi tweeted: *"To defeat Donald Trump in 2020, we need to understand why he won done in 2016. As long as Democrat party leaders dismiss and disrespect those who voted for Trump, we will lose. As president, I will bridge the partisan divide and work side-by-side with all Americans to get things."*

Trump sells ideas that the people want to own, or that make solid economic sense over the long-term – a period that transcends a "next election" psychology which dominated the Swamp Denizen approach.

For Biden to win, Tulsi Gabbard is the rational running mate. He has said he wanted a female Vice President, and he is unlikely to find one with the military experience he lacks. Tulsi's also fiscally rational – before it became Politically Correct to support money for an emergency UBI (as HR 897), which she expressed in a tweet as being "*the most simple, direct form of assistance to help weather this storm. Call your Member of Congress now to let them know why this is so important.*"

Concurrent with her work in the House, Bernie Sanders was saying: "*We must make certain that the government is getting this money into the hands of working families and the most vulnerable as quick.*"

Initially, Trump had suggested suspending payroll taxes to increase cash-in-hand. But, as we know, that put too little money into circulation – a mere 6.3% of wages, received weekly, assuming the individual's job is still there. The nature of the fight against the pandemic meant closing businesses like bars and restaurants, or any place where large numbers of people gather in close contact.

On 18 March Tulsi officially ended her campaign and threw her support behind Biden. Whether or not he'll pick a solid running mate is in question.

Biden's age is a reality we need to deal with. He is in that group that has the most virus-related deaths. Plus, Biden's draft-dodger excuse – asthma – if it was valid, then he also has the basis for the respiratory distress associated with the virus fatalities. It is possible Biden could receive the Democratic nomination and, since projections indicate the virus will still be in circulation in the fall of 2020, campaign stops could have him contract the disease.

In the meantime, as Americans were directed to cease foreign travel, and those already abroad were advised to return immediately or face the possibility of not being able to return in the near future, on 19 March it was announced that some existing malaria might be effective against Wuhan virus.

When Trump stated there could be a treatment within weeks, he was called a liar, and yet within that timeframe it was announced that existing FDA approved medications were being recommended.

Granted, the experts were saying there were improvements to be made and the drugs might not work in all cases, but Trump was proved correct – medications were available within the stated timeframe.